Advanced Technological Education

Programs at Community

Colleges

▶ ▶ ▶ ▶

The Learning Edge

EDITED BY JAMES R. MAHONEY & LYNN BARNETT

COMMUNITY COLLEGE PRESS®

a division of the American Association of Community Colleges
Washington, D.C.

3 9902 00053 5791

This book is based upon work supported by the National Science Foundation under grant number DUE-97138868 to the American Association of Community Colleges.

The editors acknowledge with gratitude the contributions of the many past and present ATE community college program directors; and thank Jennifer Henderson, and especially Ellen Hause, for their invaluable support.

The American Association of Community Colleges (AACC) is the primary advocacy organization for the nation's community colleges. The association represents 1,100 two-year, associate degree-granting institutions and some 10 million students. AACC provides leadership and service in five key areas: policy initiatives, advocacy, research, education services, and coordination/networking.

Printed in the United States of America.

ISBN 0-87117-326-3

Contents

Foreword

When Congress enacted legislation in 1993 establishing the Advanced Technological Education program, America's community colleges became the focus of a National Science Foundation effort to improve the nation's technological workforce. More opportunities appeared for community college students across the nation as new programs were developed with ATE support. The traditional open door of our community colleges opened even wider, welcoming new students seeking world-class skills in science, mathematics, engineering, and technology. The colleges had both the blessing and the financial support of the National Science Foundation, which helped students to realize their goals for exciting careers in new and emerging technical fields. By 2000, hundreds of community colleges had grown into an extraordinary network of administrators, faculty, students, and K-12 and business partners.

The Learning Edge aims to put a face on the first seven years of the ATE program by showcasing activities, partners, and achievements at 13 colleges. Comments from students, instructors, and business representatives illustrate ATE's significant impact on individuals.

For much of the last decade, NSF has raised public consciousness about the capacity of community colleges to offer strong science, mathematics, engineering, and technology education programs, and has helped the colleges push the "learning edge." This book is one of several activities supported by an NSF grant to the American Association of Community Colleges.

George R. Boggs
President
American Association of Community Colleges

Introduction

James R. Mahoney

Education reform is at the heart of the stories told in this monograph. These profiles describe the programs that 13 community colleges, along with their partners, have implemented to improve student learning. These innovative and successful programs are funded through the Advanced Technological Education (ATE) program administered by the National Science Foundation.

In distinct ways, the programs aim to reshape the model that has defined education for decades. The more ambitious programs have created an entirely new model; others have chipped away at the old one to create a more responsive approach to teaching and learning. Each of the community colleges has based its innovations on current education research, on its own considerable experience, on student feedback, and on the advice and counsel of its community partners. In creating these new approaches, each college has exhibited the kind of extraordinary courage, energy, and commitment that are demanded to successfully confront tradition.

While the programs focus on improvement in science, mathematics, engineering, and technology education, the forward-edge learning and teaching strategies they employ can be applied to all disciplines at all education levels.

About the ATE Program

The preamble to the public law that established the ATE program defines the program's broad parameters:

An Act to establish a national advanced technician training program, utilizing the resources of the Nation's two-year associate-

degree-granting colleges to expand the pool of skilled technicians in strategic advanced-technology fields, to increase the productivity of the Nation's industries, and to improve the competitiveness of the United States in international trade, and for other purposes.

The purposes stated for the program include:
- improving science and technical education at colleges that grant associate degrees
- improving secondary school and postsecondary curricula in mathematics and science
- improving the educational opportunities of postsecondary students by creating comprehensive articulation agreements and planning between two-year and four-year institutions
- promoting outreach to improve mathematics and science instruction in secondary schools

At least two characteristics distinguish this legislation. First, in very clear language, the law closely connects excellence in technical education to economic competitiveness. Second, it acknowledges the vital role that community colleges and secondary schools play in preparing a competitive workforce.

The ATE legislation, which was enacted in 1993, promotes exemplary improvement of education in technology fields by supporting curriculum development and program improvement at the undergraduate and secondary levels, especially for students of advanced technologies in order to make them successful in the high-performance workplace. Curriculum development includes the design and implementation of new curricula, courses, laboratories, and instructional materials. Program improvement encompasses faculty and teacher development, student academic support, and formal cooperative arrangements among institutions and other partners.

The aims of the ATE program are to produce major improvements in advanced technology education, create models for other institutions, ensure that students gain strong backgrounds in mathematics and science, and generate educational products that can be applied nationwide.

NSF's Division of Undergraduate Education (DUE) and Division of Elementary, Secondary, and Informal Education (ESIE) jointly manage the ATE program.

From its inception through the end of fiscal year 1999, the ATE program supported more than 250 individual projects and 12 national centers of excellence. The centers focus on specific technologies and serve as national resources that provide wide-ranging support to all institutions that are concerned about improvement in those specific technologies. Total ATE funds available during the first years of the program's life (FY 1993 to FY 1999) were approximately $150 million, with an additional $3 million contributed by related NSF programs. These numbers may not look extraordinary in an era of billion-dollar federal programs, but when it is understood that these funds are aimed primarily at supporting community college activities, the amounts become remarkable. Before the emergence of the ATE program, NSF channeled approximately $200,000 to community colleges in the first few years of the 1990s.

The special activities that the ATE program supports include those conducted by the American Association of Community Colleges. AACC's role is to provide intensive opportunities for program participants and their partners to network with one another and to share the program's interests and accomplishments with educators and business partners across the nation, especially community colleges. The ATE program's success and the exceptional reputation that the NSF enjoys on Capitol Hill ensure that the program will continue to grow.

About These Stories

This book emphasizes the human aspects of the 13 profiled programs by underscoring students' experience. Students are the center of all learning efforts in these programs: their preparation for meaningful places in the high-tech workplace, their involvement

in their own education experiences, their application of classroom learning to the realities of the workplace, their recognition of connections across disciplines, their responsibilities as teammates, and their role in improving the programs. The students are not mere containers to be filled with the knowledge and experience of trained faculty. They are, rather, full partners in a practical learning environment, with valuable perspectives and ideas to contribute to the enterprise. This view explains the use of learning communities as well as the emphasis on real work-world problem solving. It also explains why the programs use "just-in-time" learning (rather than the traditional approach of presenting materials according to an artificial schedule) and why they use advanced technology as both a teaching tool and an industrial application. In many of the ATE programs described here, faculty serve as learning facilitators rather than the classroom overseers of previous eras.

Key to these programs is the belief that basic skills instruction cannot be isolated in one course or another but must be taught and emphasized in all courses. Skills such as communication, computation, analysis, problem solving, and application are part of all instruction; that's why team teaching and cross-discipline collaboration are important components of these programs. It's also part of the reason for emphasis on faculty development. Faculty must be able to release students' native intelligence and involve them in their own learning. These underlying principles apply to any technical discipline.

Who Can Benefit from This Book

This book describes the plans, achievements, and processes of each of the featured ATE programs; it does not evaluate them. The stories are important to everyone interested in increasing student achievement, in preparing capable workers for present and future economies, in stimulating a commitment and belief in lifelong learning, and in enhancing personal development. Consider the following groups and approaches:

Educators. The ATE programs described here illustrate how new learning approaches can be applied in the classroom and what their outcomes have been so far. They identify new curricula in a variety of formats using a selection of appropriate technology to accelerate and buttress learning.

The stories speak to the K–12 system, to community colleges, and to four-year colleges and universities.

Employers. Both public- and private-sector employers can see how their active involvement in designing education programs and setting the direction they will take is welcomed and appreciated by educators. In every instance described here, employers have played vital and varied roles in the program's success.

Legislators. For legislators at all levels of government, the profiles identify the kinds of programs and learning systems that work and the kinds of efforts that deserve to be supported through legislation and appropriations. They communicate an optimism that can address the nagging problems of unsatisfactory student achievement and students' lack of readiness for the next steps toward work or additional schooling. The stories document the existence of talented and committed education professionals, now working in American schools and colleges, who are capable of leading successful education reform.

National leaders. Leaders in professional societies and in national education and industry associations will find that the ATE programs described include examples of activities they can encourage and support. Leaders can exercise their commitment to education reform by sharing these success stories with their organizations' members and by encouraging the members to participate in ATE programs.

Government agencies. These NSF-supported programs can serve as a model for activities that other agencies might support. People in schools and colleges across the country have an abundance of creativity and ideas; only the release of seed money is needed to put those ideas to work improving student learning and achievement.

The profiles presented here describe programs in which ongoing change occurs. Creating new learning schemes using current research, applying and assessing those schemes, and revising them based on results take hard work and time. One of the most significant features of these 13 programs is that all of them have vowed to continue the process beyond the life of their federal grants.

What the Programs Have Achieved

Over their five-year history, the programs have covered multiple disciplines. The profiles include references to most of the following disciplines:

- manufacturing
- information technology
- environmental science
- physics
- mathematics
- agriculture
- chemistry
- metrology/machine tooling
- engineering
- science
- multidisciplinary programs

Three of the profiles describe professional development programs that stress a variety of disciplines.

The programs have produced an impressive range of outcomes, from new and revised courses and degree programs to new standards and professional development opportunities. The emphasis on faculty development activities has several purposes. In one instance, it's designed to change the way science, mathematics, engineering, and technology are taught in community colleges throughout the state, by using innovative instructional principles and

Sample ATE Program Outcomes
The 13 programs described in this report achieved the following outcomes:
- new courses in telecommunications
- new course units in math and physics
- new course modules in physics
- new courses and laboratory demonstrations in environmental science
- new curricula in agriculture and food technology
- new associate in applied science (AAS) degree programs in advanced process operations and distinctive manufacturing technology
- new AAS degree and certificate programs in environmental technology
- skill standards for information technology
- faculty development in a variety of areas: geographical information systems, image processing, remote sensing; learning/teaching innovation in interdisciplinary studies; computer network training, environmental sciences, information technology, and telecommunications

strategies. In another case, faculty development is aimed at building a state cadre of community college and high school instructors who are experts at teaching computer network technology and at using the technology for instruction. The three ATE centers of excellence described in this book offer faculty development opportunities as a means of sharing the latest approaches in their fields with faculty from across the country, which in turn encourages improvement nationwide.

Partners

ATE grantees are required to establish partnerships with groups that can help them achieve project goals. While partnerships were already a way of life for community colleges, the demands of these ATE activities enriched the variety and intensity of such relationships. In the course of the program, long-standing connections were strengthened and new ones created. All of these connections were influenced by the language in the NSF program guidelines:

> To be effective, technological education programs require partnerships among two- and four-year colleges, universities, secondary schools, business, government, and industry.

The guiding principle that encourages close connections among community colleges, secondary schools, and four-year colleges and universities is that education, to be effective, must be treated as a continuum. A "fix" in one part of the system may be negligible and short-lived if the other parts don't anticipate and prepare for it. Secondary school students must be prepared in math and science and must be aware of what will be expected of them in higher education institutions if they are to move smoothly from one level to another. Community college students must be aware of what will be required of them if they continue on toward a higher degree. Colleges and universities should help to develop channels that lead students smoothly from one level to another, and should devise formal articulation agreements that encourage community college students to continue on to the baccalaureate level. All of the programs presented in this book have been successful in such efforts.

Secondary school partners. Many of the community colleges have enhanced their relationships with secondary schools by expanding existing tech prep programs. Middle and high school colleagues serve on faculty training teams, work on curriculum committees to synchronize high school classes with community college programs, co-host science and math awareness events, and are joining college advisory committees.

Other higher education partners. Four-year colleges and universities have partnered with community colleges in a variety of ways. Some have worked with the community colleges to establish responsive articulation agreements. Others have, together with the community colleges, designed laboratory demonstrations, created real-world problem sets, arranged internships and other work experiences for students, and made advanced laboratory equipment and facilities available to students. In each of these projects, four-year colleges and universities have contributed advice about curriculum design and content, research on the learning and teaching processes, and material and personnel resources that could support the program. In a few cases, a four-year institution has provided project leadership, serving as either principal investigator or as co-principal investigator. In one case, representatives of the institution served on curriculum preparation teams and wrote one of a set of modules for a curriculum. Four-year institutions have played an active role on the national visiting committees organized by NSF to help with and review the work of some of the larger projects, and on the local project advisory boards.

Employer partners. Collaborative relationships with employers, public and private, have been vital to many of these projects. One of the principal dimensions of the ATE program is to convert the classroom into a real-world environment. Employers provide the substance for this conversion, and their contributions have been varied and significant. They have permitted faculty to examine their workplaces, and employees to participate on curriculum-building teams. Employers have sat on curriculum development committees, sometimes through the designing-a-curriculum (DACUM) process. They have helped devise problem sets for classroom use. They have arranged for students to have experiences that acquaint them with the workplace, including internships, shadowing opportunities, and tours. They have made cutting-edge technology available to the colleges for instruction, and have served as instructors or tutors in some programs. Their expertise has helped create standards in skill areas that were lacking standards. They have served on project advisory committees, and have spoken about the project to different audiences, including other employers. They have shared contact and resource information with project officials. In several cases, they have contributed materials, equipment, software, and funds to help the projects exceed their original goals.

Other community college partners. Along with other unusual relationships, the program has stimulated relationships among community colleges themselves. In spite of their reputation for effective collaboration with an assortment of education and noneducation organizations, it is uncommon for community colleges to collaborate with other community colleges, especially those outside their geographic region. The ATE program has triggered a number of such relationships. In several instances, community colleges have become cooperating institutions that share responsibility for various aspects of a grant program. In some cases, partners assume responsibility for creating new courses or course modules, or for serving as test sites for refining new materials. In other cases, they serve as lead institutions for offering faculty development in a specific technology for which they are noted. In all cases, the cooperating institutions are connected electronically through e-mail, Web sites, or videoconferencing, which lets them communicate with each other immediately and responsively.

Unexpected Outcomes

As with other types of pilot programs, the ones profiled here experienced some surprises. Nearly all the colleges reported that their relationships with partners improved noticeably because of the ATE program. These partners included four-year colleges and universities, employers, government agencies, and K–12 school systems. While new partnerships were forged during the program, many of the relationships that existed earlier were enriched and strengthened. Chemeketa Community College staff, for example, discovered that the ATE program had reduced or eliminated barriers to cooperation that had inhibited education innovation in the past. Many of the colleges found that program endeavors had a positive effect on a number of areas in which there had been tensions in the past:

- General education faculty and technical faculty teamed up.
- Community colleges from different locations freely shared information and ideas.
- Staff members from four-year colleges, universities, and community colleges developed respectful liaisons.
- Community colleges and high schools collaborated effectively.
- High schools interacted more directly with their communities.
- Relationships between community colleges and local employers intensified and expanded.

The reporting colleges offered no explanations for these phenomena, but apparently all these partners recognized both the importance of program goals and their own interest in program outcomes. One of the programs' primary interests is to clarify the interconnectedness of academic disciplines; another is to acknowledge the relationship between education excellence and the health of communities, economies, and social institutions. The programs focused on specific tasks designed to respond to clearly defined needs. The program's success depended on each partner making an effective contribution. Another explanation for the programs' success is that the leaders were committed to achieving positive reform by changing old patterns.

The colleges reported other unanticipated changes:

- Interest in incorporating technology in instruction spread to other departments in the colleges.
- New learning and teaching approaches were adopted in courses and departments that weren't part of the programs.
- Teaching effectiveness improved.
- Using teams for curriculum development enhanced participants' leadership skills.
- New learning and teaching approaches energized faculty members, some of whom postponed retirement.
- New learning and teaching approaches excited students, contributed to the retention of high-risk students, and increased enrollment.

The staff at one college, however, noted a drawback: It was surprisingly difficult to secure paid internships for program students. Employers were happy to hire graduates but reluctant to support paid student internships.

Outside Buy-In to the Programs

A project's impressiveness is sometimes measured by the leveraged funds it has generated. If that measure were applied to these 13 programs, most would prove extremely impressive. Not including the important matching funds that the each institution committed to its program (which in some cases approached 50 percent), some of the colleges received donations of cash, equipment, software, and materials valued at many thousands of dollars.

What stands out in this category is the diversity of leveraged funds reported by the colleges. Four offered no figures. One, Bellevue Community College, received donations totaling more than $11 million. Other colleges reported additional support that ranged from a single $10,000 corporate grant (from Hughes Missile Systems to Pima Community College) to combined donations totaling $750,000 (from John Deere Company, the college, and software firms to Hawkeye Community College). The largest contributions came from private firms, including software companies; the colleges or college foundations (contributions beyond the required grant matches); and state government offices.

The more successful colleges have certain characteristics in common. They have long-standing, successful relationships with the corporations that made donations; the colleges and the corporations respect each other's interests and capabilities. The colleges are often major trainers of new employees and serve as resources for retraining current workers. Sometimes the relationship is even more intimate because college staff members are former employees of a firm or because adjunct faculty are full-time workers at the firm. Corporate policies include support for local education institutions and for lifelong learning for employees. The proximity of the colleges and the businesses makes collaboration both easy and natural. The colleges often have experienced and accomplished grant development staff members who aggressively seek additional funding to support college efforts. Project staff involve corporate sponsors in important aspects of the program and make it clear to the firms that the program's success will be of practical benefit to them. Both parties appreciate the mutual benefits and the appropriateness of the partnership. Of course, none of these characteristics would be enough if the college did not have a high-quality product to "sell."

Influences on Program Development

The National Science Foundation's intention from the inception of the ATE program was to create an interactive national network of leadership colleges whose imprint and achievement would be bolstered by mutual support. College staff members' responses to surveys suggest that ATE has served this purpose. Connections with other ATE-funded projects and the centers of excellence were the most frequently identified resources. Various skill standards (including those of the Secretary's Commission on Achieving Necessary Skills [SCANS], NSF-produced standards, and American Chemical Society standards) served as additional resources. Other influences on network building were the work, meetings, and publications of professional associations and societies. Additional resources identified by the 13 featured colleges include college consortia whose members worked directly on project activities; thinkers and leaders of education reform; private firms with expertise in multimedia presentations, curriculum design, and software applications; and evaluators, consultants, and advisory committees. National ATE conferences and other NSF-sponsored meetings supplemented these efforts. Meetings were designed to connect principal investigators and their partners, and to provide opportunities for colleges to share their work with others, to talk and think about issues central to the program, and to identify additional resources that would help ensure success.

Student Recruitment

Some of the 13 community colleges profiled here reported that the ATE program was creating new materials for standard courses in which recruitment was not a problem. Recruiting students to new programs can be difficult. In some cases, the colleges have used standard, although very active and generally comprehensive, strategies to involve students in their programs, such as visiting local high schools. College representatives have talked with high school administrators, academic advisors, counselors, and faculty about their programs, and have made presentations at high school career days and college career expositions. Some have exposed young students to the ATE programs through connections made through high school tech prep programs.

Other, not-so-traditional, approaches have been used to attract student attention, including program flyers, newspaper and radio ads, Web announcements, and information seminars at employer sites. Hoping to inspire middle school students, some of the colleges have participated in state events that focus on science and math careers. They have co-hosted or hosted field demonstrations of cutting-edge technologies. Oklahoma State University-Okmulgee, the state's technical college, offers two-week summer manufacturing academies that are open to middle school students from across the state, and that provide leadership training to rising ninth graders who serve as mentors in the academies.

At the collegiate level, OSU-Okmulgee also offers scholarships to students who enroll in its Distinctive Manufacturing Technology program, and offers finders' fees to students who recruit others. Recruitment numbers jumped considerably when Northwest Indian College set up information tables in two reservation stores. Program staff hired and trained local monitors to manage the tables and to explain the program to prospective students. In many places, once a class was established, student word-of-mouth endorsement served as an effective recruiting tool.

Program Recognition

In order to extend the reach of education reform through these programs, each college was expected to disseminate information about its activities to local audiences, as well as to other colleges and universities. Professional societies were also targeted.

The exposure given these projects over their short lifetimes has been extraordinary. It is testimony to the programs' quality, to their importance, and to the chord they strike in people who are concerned about the issues and academic disciplines involved. The exposure has taken many forms. Most frequently, project staff gave presentations or conducted workshops about their efforts at local, regional, and national meetings sponsored by professional organizations. The programs have been

the focus of articles in professional journals and books, and of local newspaper stories. As a result of the programs, the 13 community colleges have formed formal articulation agreements with four-year colleges and universities, professional organizations have certified and formally endorsed curricula, and discipline-specific groups have granted accreditation to programs. Some colleges have attracted additional funds from an assortment of sources. College staff members have been given awards for their leadership, teaching, faculty development, and mentoring. Faculty members have received fellowships related to their work and staff members have provided consulting services to other colleges. The U.S. Department of Commerce has used two of the 13 colleges to host regional town hall meetings on information technology issues.

What's Next?

All of the colleges profiled in this book plan to continue their work beyond their NSF grant funding. They will test and refine their courses and curricula and make them known to other groups; offer workshops to help train faculty from other institutions; and expand the program's reach into other courses and disciplines. Some of the colleges expect to seek additional funding to support these activities; others plan to continue their work as part of their usual college duties. At least two of the colleges plan to become self-sufficient by selling their services and products in the commercial marketplace. One college, in addition to continuing and expanding its current program, anticipates playing a major role in a new, handsomely funded state program that has a component centered on environmental science education and training. Other continuation activities that the colleges plan include expanding the program into a four-year degree curriculum, organizing train-the-trainer workshops, coordinating paid student internships and cooperative education experiences, conducting faculty conferences, producing multimedia curriculum products, developing credit-for-experience programs for employed workers, integrating technology into other courses and disciplines, creating interactive Web sites, using the state distance-learning network to share program results and to continue program efforts, expanding workplace research activities, and sponsoring national conferences.

Typically, the great fear about federally funded programs is that, once the funds dry up, the program will end and the work will be shelved. That is not likely to happen with the ATE program.

DEVELOPING NEW PROGRAMS
Lessons Learned
- **Planning**
  - View a new grant or program as a business start-up.
  - Overestimate the time expected to complete tasks.
  - Identify clearly the duties, responsibilities, and expectations of all staff and partners.
  - Plan sufficient time for administrative functions (budgeting, accounting, reporting, and managing).
  - Plan for sustainability and develop organizational change strategies early.
- **Staffing**
  - Provide release time for project leaders and for faculty members rewriting curriculum.
  - Budget for staff support.
  - Focus on full-time faculty assigned to single departments.
  - Locate all program staff as closely together as possible.
- **Faculty**
  - Find ways for faculty to experience the workplace.
  - Provide writing support for technical faculty.
- **Students**
  - Recruit students early.
  - Find student scholarship money.
  - Confirm business commitments for internships and cooperative education experiences.
- **Accountability**
  - Use outside experts to create assessment instruments and procedures.
  - Involve mid-level managers in collegewide efforts.
  - Offer grant administration training to college budget officers.
  - Focus on a few activities and assess them well.

Recommendations
The profiled colleges were invited to comment on what they would do differently were they to begin their ATE programs again. A common theme was the need for planning—especially upfront planning, time management, staffing requirements, and grant expectations. One college said that managing the grant was like running a new business, with all of the attendant problems and pressures. The collective comments may be viewed as preliminary "lessons learned."

Conclusion
Our hope is that readers will be intrigued by these brief descriptions of exemplary college programs and will contact the project principals for further information. The programs have worked well in these institutions, and we believe they will work well in other colleges.

South Carolina Technical College System
Columbia, South Carolina

South Carolina Advanced Technological Education (SC ATE) Exemplary Faculty Project

▶ **FOCUS**
▶ Faculty as catalysts in statewide teaching and curriculum reform
▶ Math, science, communications, and engineering

College Environment

The South Carolina Technical College System, established in 1961, is governed by the South Carolina State Board for Technical and Comprehensive Education. The system comprises 16 two-year technical colleges located throughout the Palmetto State, a comprehensive continuing education program in which citizens can continually upgrade their skills, and a specialized business and industry training program called Special Schools. The system is fundamentally committed to the support of economic development in South Carolina and serves as a catalyst for economic growth in the state. Its mission is to ensure the economic and human resource development of the state through:

- training assistance to new and expanding businesses and industries
- occupational and technical training through continuing education programs
- college credit pre-baccalaureate education

More than 200,000 people annually take advantage of some type of course or training through the state's technical college system. In the past 10 years, system-wide enrollment has increased by 50 percent. Thirty-eight percent of all undergraduate students in South Carolina

South Carolina Technical College System
South Carolina ATE Center of Excellence
111 Executive Center Drive
Columbia, SC 29210
Ph: 803/896-5280
www.state.sc.us/teched/stbrd.htm
Executive Director: James L. Hudgins

Contacts
Lynn G. Mack, Principal Investigator
Mathematics Instructor
Piedmont Technical College
Ph: 864/941-8449
Fax: 864/941-8691
E-mail: Mack_L@ped.tec.sc.us

Elaine L. Craft, Co-principal Investigator
Director, SC ATE Center of Excellence
SC State Board for Technical and Comprehensive Education
Ph: 803/896-5410
Fax: 803/896-5409
E-mail: crafte@sbt.tec.sc.us

James C. Wood, Ph.D., Co-principal Investigator
Division Chair, Industrial and Engineering Technology
Tri-County Technical College
Ph: 864/646-8361, ext. 2176
Fax: 864/646-8256
E-mail: jwood@tricty.tricounty.tec.sc.us

Program Web Address
www.scate.org

are enrolled in a technical college, just 4 percent fewer than are enrolled in four-year institutions. Twenty-eight percent of all high school graduates enter the South Carolina Technical College System. Nearly a third of the students are 30 years old or older, and women compose nearly 60 percent of the students. More than half of the state's minority student population is enrolled in a technical college. The system employs more than 3,000 full- and part-time faculty.

South Carolina continued its record-breaking economic development streak in 1998 and was first among Southeastern states with business investments totaling $5.8 billion. Since 1995, the state's economy has grown by more than $22 billion in capital investment, which has created more than 100,000 new jobs. The state is experiencing an influx of major manufacturers, especially in information technology, which is leading to an even greater demand for qualified technicians. South Carolina's population is becoming more diverse as the Hispanic population grows.

Program Profile

The South Carolina Advanced Technological Education (SC ATE) program is a statewide initiative instituted in 1995 and dedicated to increasing the quantity, quality, and diversity of engineering technology graduates—through the state's 16 technical colleges—to support economic development in

Piedmont Technical College (Greenwood, SC) ATE faculty member (Gordon Campbell, now dean of engineering and industrial technology) responds to team questions. Piedmont was one of three South Carolina technical colleges that pilot-tested the new SC ATE Technology Gateway (also known as pre-engineering technology) semester curriculum in fall 1998.

Technical college graduates that I have hired have been able to hit the ground running! These graduates are generally able to generate revenue for my corporation sooner than those with a comparable four-year degree. I feel that the SC ATE program will do nothing but improve the quality of these graduates in the future.
—South Carolina business manager

South Carolina. The program emphasizes collaborative teaching strategies and extensive active-learning techniques, in conjunction with faculty and student teamwork. It is funded jointly by the National Science Foundation and the South Carolina State Board for Technical and Comprehensive Education and managed by three principal investigators under the auspices of the state board. The program is proving that exemplary faculty can lead grassroots, systemic educational reform.

The SC ATE Exemplary Faculty Project laid the groundwork for the SC ATE Center of Excellence by preparing a cadre of ATE faculty at each of the 16 technical colleges. The faculty's job was to provide local leadership of the center, which trains faculty to use a variety of research-based teaching strategies to respond more effectively to the diverse learning needs of students and create a model of the workplace. The Exemplary Faculty Project work was progressively integrated into the ATE Center of Excellence, whose mission is to increase the quantity, quality and diversity of engineering technology graduates. The center identified four critical success factors or essential accomplishments to guide its work:
- continuing development of pre-engineering technology and first-year engineering technology curricula
- faculty development that supports the most effective teaching methodologies and creating learning environments that model the workplace
- recruitment and retention of students, particularly women and minorities

• development of a statewide model for creating a seamless pipeline for educational opportunities for students to become well-qualified engineering technology technicians

Interdisciplinary teams of mathematics, science (primarily physics), communication, and technology faculty deliver new curricula developed through the ATE center. The curricula is integrated and problem-based, and requires student teams to function in a setting that reflects the workplace. Project activities in 1995-98 focused on:

• conducting workshops and other professional development opportunities focused on teaming principles, application of instructional technology, multiple intelligences theory, learning styles, cooperative learning/active learning, problem-based learning, and assessment
• organizing interdisciplinary faculty teams from mathematics, science, technology, and communication disciplines
• facilitating research projects in which interdisciplinary faculty teams designed courses or course components
• sponsoring workplace research to enable faculty to bring industry techniques and problem situations and solutions into the classroom, making the instruction more reality-based
• creating networks for collaboration across departments and campuses (these communications networks support faculty sharing and learning)
• creating classroom environments that reflect conditions in the workplace

As the faculty development program matured within SC ATE, program leaders directed more attention to piloting the ATE Scholars program for students in fall 1999. With assistance from sponsoring companies, this program provides students with a real-world work experience. The scholars program is endorsed and actively supported by the South Carolina Department of Commerce and the South Carolina Technology Alliance. Back in the classroom, faculty find that students in the ATE Scholars program are more likely than other students to graduate.

PARTNERS

Business, industry, government, and academic partners provided support for the project through the donation of professional expertise and personnel time.

AMP, Inc. Provided a corporate representative to serve on the National Visiting Committee (a national advisory committee attached to the project), a manufacturing plant manager to serve on the project Advisory Board (a statewide advisory panel), and electrical and mechanical engineers to work on curriculum development teams.

South Carolina Technical Colleges. Contributed computer equipment for project faculty, hosted project events on their campuses, and piloted and implemented new pre-engineering courses.

College foundations. Funded special activities for project faculty and various events. Example: the Orangeburg-Calhoun Technical College Foundation doubled grant support for local project faculty participating in workplace research, providing faculty stipends for the college's team to conduct research on engineering technicians in industry. The college supplemented the foundation's donation.

South Carolina Department of Commerce. Supports ATE Scholars Program.

South Carolina Technology Alliance. Supports ATE Scholars Program.

Advisory board. Provides advice and consultation. Corporate, government, and higher education members include representatives of Robert Bosch Corporation; Carolina Trucks & Equipment, Inc.; The Citadel; Clemson University; Exxon Research & Engineering Company (Annandale, New Jersey); Michelin North America, Inc.; National Dropout Prevention Center (Clemson University); Policy Management Systems Corporation; South Carolina State University; South Carolina Department of Education; Solectron Corporation; South Carolina ETV; University of South Carolina; and the Virginia Community College System.

Academy for Educational Development, Inc. Provides evaluation services to the project.

MAJOR ACHIEVEMENTS

Exemplary faculty. A cadre of 87 faculty representing 16 technical colleges in the state and four major disciplines—mathematics, science, communications/English, and engineering technology—were trained to design and use new integrated, problem-based curricular materials and teaching methods.

Faculty development. Three faculty retreats and seven major professional development events have been held. The retreats and professional-development program topics included problem-based learning, institutional effectiveness, multiple intelligences, active learning, teaming, instructional technology, assessment, and peer group review among other central issues. National experts served as instructors.

Workplace research model. A workplace research model was developed to assist teams of interdisciplinary faculty when they visited industries to gather information on workplace skills and environment.

Roundtables. This professional development activity was initiated to provide a forum for project faculty to share with and mentor other faculty in the state technical-college system over a distance learning teleconferencing system. More than 300 faculty, in addition to ATE program faculty, have participated.

Outreach. Program faculty prepared and conducted more than 70 presentations/workshops for local, state, and national audiences.

Curriculum development. Project faculty created curriculum materials employing innovative principles. The materials incorporate the four disciplines targeted by the project.

ATE scholars. With state and corporate support, students gain work experience while still in their engineering technology program.

There is no way I would go back to the way I used to teach.
                                    —ATE *faculty member*

Why This Approach?

South Carolina was facing several problems in engineering technology that program designers hoped to solve. In the engineering technology programs, colleges faced insufficient diversity among students—85 percent of students in engineering technology programs were white males. Not many students succeeded: attrition rates approached 80 or 90 percent in some programs. Educational research within the South Carolina technical colleges and elsewhere showed a mismatch between traditional teaching approaches and new learning designs that include contextual learning, learning styles, working in teams, and problem-centered learning. There was a lack of connection and collaboration between faculty who teach different disciplines to students in the engineering technology program. And courses were not being taken in a logical order.

The Exemplary Faculty Project addresses the need for systemic change to increase the quantity, quality, and diversity of engineering technology graduates in the state and nation by:

- restructuring the learning environment and preparing two-year technical college students to compete in today's high-performance global marketplace
- implementing an integrated, problem-based engineering technology curriculum
- evaluating and disseminating successful practices and processes at the local, state and national levels

Influences on Program Development

The program used a large collection of resources to provide faculty with the intellectual and pedagogical foundations required to support innovation. These resources included books, videotapes, and presentations from specialists in a variety of fields. Information on videotapes and experts may be obtained from the Center's office or the SC ATE Web site (www.scate.org). Resource books distributed to faculty appear at the end of the chapter.

Students were excited [by the new approach], and I haven't seen that in a while.

—*ATE faculty member*

Faculty Recruitment

For each college in the system, the project management team developed a selection process that included a poster to announce the program, information packets for potential applicants, an information video, and selection and evaluation criteria for use by applicants and supervisors making the final team selections. In the initial year, 61 faculty were chosen for the multi-discipline teams of mathematics, physical science, communications, and engineering technology.

In addition, each college was invited to nominate up to four faculty alternates for inclusion. Alternates were selected using the same criteria as those used for the faculty teams. Eighteen alternates were enrolled in the program and worked in teams, shared responsibility for project outcomes, and participated in all professional development activities.

Unexpected Outcomes

Three significant unexpected outcomes occurred in the program. First, a focus on faculty teams and team leadership helped faculty to develop leadership skills. Among other things, faculty members learned how to design and conduct effective presentations for adult audiences by using PowerPoint and other software. Partially as a result of their leadership in the program, many faculty involved with the program received promotions. They now serve as vice presidents for instruction, division deans, department heads, committee chairs, and team leaders.

Second, although a few faculty members left the program, the anticipated attrition of 50 participants in the second and third years of the grant did not occur. Between 1995, when the program began, and 1998, the active number of faculty grew from 75 to 87. Since 1998, additional faculty from both technical colleges and high schools across the state have become involved through the SC ATE Center of Excellence. In summer of 2000, the number of faculty/teacher participants was 110 and continuing to grow.

Third, faculty commitment to the project was greater than expected. Some faculty who were ready to retire or suffering from burnout became reinvigorated and no longer wish to quit teaching. Reportedly, these instructors now enjoy the classroom more and understand better how to address the learning needs of their students. Changes in classroom methodology demonstrate the faculty's desire to meet such needs and a commitment to change.

Recognition

The Exemplary Faculty Project has gained widespread recognition. The principal investigator received the 2000 Governor's Award for Excellence in Science Awareness in acknowledgement of the importance of SC ATE's work in recruiting, retaining, and graduating students in engineering technology programs. In 1998, SC ATE won the David Pierce Leadership Award in the team category from the National Institute for Leadership and Institutional Effectiveness. The team award is presented to community college teams and their partners from K-12, higher education, business and industry, and state and federal government who are working to improve community college effectiveness.

Other major awards and nominations were received in 1998. *Out of the Box*—an Exemplary Faculty Project guide with accompanying video—

Florence-Darlington Technical College (Florence, SC) ATE students work in teams to determine what they know and what they need to know to solve a real-world industry problem. These students were part of the 1999-2000 SC ATE first-year engineering technology core classes at the college. Hands-on learning opportunities involve students and enable them to apply what they are learning. With the ATE curriculum, the question "Why am I learning this" is answered every day.

Classroom environment has improved, but what has been most spectacular is the increased student retention.

—ATE faculty member

was selected as a top-10 finalist for the 1998 Bellwether Award in Instructional Programs and Services. The Bellwether Awards, sponsored by the Institute of Higher Education at the University of Florida, acknowledge excellence and innovation in community college programming. In addition, the state board presented the project's principal investigator with the A. Wade Martin Innovator of the Year Award—the most prestigious honor presented annually to a South Carolina technical college educator. The award recognizes individuals in the technical college system who employ innovative approaches to meet the ever-changing needs in technical education and whose achievements assist in statewide economic development and the education of students. The SC ATE Center of Excellence received the 1998 National Leadership Forum Achievement Award for Outstanding Partnership. A third award came from Jobs for the Future for the center's outstanding contribution in advancing the development of work, learning, and citizenship.

Tri-County Technical College (Pendleton, SC) ATE faculty member (Ron Talley, department head, electronics engineering technology) works with a student team during pilot-testing of the SC ATE first-year engineering technology (ET) core curriculum. Tri-County and Florence-Darlington Technical Colleges pilot tested the ET core during the 1998-99 academic year.

Thus far program staff have made approximately 75 related presentations to local, state, and national audiences, reaching well over 2,000 educators and others. They also presented an invited paper, "Shaping a Curriculum from Workplace Research," at the 1998 American Society for Engineering Education conference.

College Commitment

All 16 colleges within the state's technical college system have actively participated in the project. It has been supported by the SC State Board for Technical and Comprehensive Education, the President's Council (composed of the chief executive officer of each college), and the Chief Instructional Officers' Peer Group (composed of the vice president for instruction from each of the colleges). In addition to significant financial support, the state technical college system made available to program participants an electronic communications network that includes computer connectivity, Internet access, and a video-conferencing system (TechNet). At least half of the state's technical colleges are implementing the technology gateway (pre-engineering) core courses and the engineering technology core courses.

Leveraged Funds

Conservative estimates suggest that the ATE program has leveraged more than $250,000 to date. Funds have come from the South Carolina State Board for Technical and Comprehensive Education (approximately $120,000); individual college contributions for equipment, space renovation/facilities, personnel, etc. (more than $100,000); individual college foundation donations; and industry partners.

What's Next?

Program faculty will continue to assist with the design and implementation of curriculum models for engineering technology in the state's technical colleges. They continue to share methodology, best practices, and research over the technical-college-system distance learning network. Presentations and workshops will expand on classroom strategies focused more on being "guides on the side" rather than on being traditional lecturers. Many plan to serve as mentors for new

ATE teaching teams. Additional workplace research is planned.

Materials Produced by the Program

Materials, available upon request from the project web site, include:

Curriculum Materials

Technology Gateway Competencies (Mathematics, Physics/Technology, Communication)

Project 1: Introduction to Technology Careers
Project 2: Mechanical—Simple Machines
Project 3: Electrical—Basic Electricity
Project 4-A: Optics
Project 4-B: Optics
Project 5: Thermal—Temperature Measuring Devices
Project 6: Fluids—Hydraulic Jack

Engineering Technology (ET) Core Courses, 1st Term

Student Competencies

Project 1: Resistance
Project 2: Current
Project 3: Voltage
Project 4: Capacitance
Project 5: Motors

Engineering Technology (ET) Core Courses, 2nd Term

Mechanical and Fluids Competencies

C.1: Rate in Linear Systems
C.2: Forces in Linear Systems
C.3: Conservation Principles
C.4: Rate in Rotational Systems
C.5: Torque in Rotational Systems
C.6: Conservation Concepts in Rotational Systems
C.7: Effective Team and Communication Skills
D.1: Density
D.2: Pressure
D.3: Archimedes' Principle
D.4: Fluid Flow
D.5: Advanced Fluid Concepts

Engineering Technology (ET) Core Courses, 3rd Term

Optics and Materials Competencies

F.1: Reflections
F.2: Refraction
F.3: Diffraction/Interference
G.1: Materials

Training class model for faculty and institutional users of the SC ATE curriculum—designed in a problem-based format; first taught in spring 1999.

Newsletter

SC ATE Center of Excellence Briefs

Reports and Presentations

Out of the box: A guide to faculty development for reform of engineering technology education in two-year technical colleges. 1997. Columbia, S.C.: SC Advanced Technological Education Exemplary Faculty Project, SC State Board for Technical and Comprehensive Education (accompanying videotape).

Mack, Lynn G., Thomas V. Mecca, and Sara Smith. 1998. *Shaping a curriculum from workplace research.* Paper presented at the 1998 American Society of Engineering Education annual conference.

Roundtable responsibility list and presentation suggestions. 1998. Columbia, S.C.: SC Advanced Technological Education Exemplary Faculty Project, SC State Board for Technical and Comprehensive Education.

Wood, James C., and Lynn G. Mack. 1997. *The impact of interdisciplinary faculty teams on engineering technology curricula.* Annual Conference Proceedings of the American Society of Engineering Education.

Workplace research: A model for South Carolina's technical college system. 1998. Columbia, S.C.: SC Advanced Technological Education Exemplary Faculty Project, South Carolina State Board for Technical and Comprehensive Education.

References

Angelo, T., and K. P. Cross. 1993. *Classroom assessment techniques.* 2d ed. San Francisco: Jossey-Bass.

Arcaro, J. F. 1995. *Teams in education: Creating an integrated approach.* Delray Beach, Fla.: St. Lucie Press.

Campbell, W. E., and K. A. Smith, eds. 1997. *New paradigms for college teaching*. Edina, Minn.: Interaction Book Co.

Fogarty, R. 1997. *Problem-based learning and other curriculum models for the multiple intelligences classroom*. Arlington Heights, Ill.: IRI Skylight Training & Publishing.

Johnson, D. W., and R. T. Johnson. 1996. *Meaningful and manageable assessment through cooperative learning*. Edina, Minn.: Interaction Book Co.

Johnson, D. W., R. T. Johnson, and K. A. Smith. 1991. *Active learning: Cooperation in the college classroom*. Edina, Minn.: Interaction Book Co.

Starfield, A. M., K. A. Smith, and A. L. Bleloch. 1994. *How to model it: Problem solving for the computer age*. Edina, Minn.: Burgess International Group.

Wilkerson, L., and W. H. Gijselaers, eds. 1996. *Bringing problem-based learning to higher education: Theory and practice*. New directions for teaching and learning, ed. R. J. Menges, no. 68. San Francisco: Jossey-Bass.

Chemeketa Community College
Salem, Oregon

Northwest Center for
Sustainable Resources (NCSR)

▶ FOCUS
▸ Curriculum modules for sustainable
  ecosystem management
▸ Summer training institutes for high
  school and college faculty

College Environment

Chemeketa Community College opened in 1969, was fully accredited in 1972, and serves four counties (spread over more than 2,600 square miles) in Oregon's Mid-Willamette Valley. The area includes Salem, the state capital—which is defined by state government and high tech industries—as well as surrounding rural communities, defined by agriculture and forestry-based industries. The college has a 194-acre main campus in North Salem and four outreach campuses. The college employs more than 245 full-time faculty and offers more than 40 professional/technical programs, college transfer courses, and developmental skill building and lifelong learning. In 1998-99, total unduplicated student headcount was 48,000, with 11,800 students enrolled full time. In 1999, the average student age was 33 years, and 55 percent of students were female. Enrollment by ethnic group was 62.7 percent white, non-Hispanic; 11.6 percent Hispanic; 3 percent Asian/Pacific Islander; 1.5 percent Native American or Alaskan Native; 0.8 percent black, non-Hispanic. Twenty percent of students did not report an ethnic group. During the past decade, Hispanic student enrollment has more than tripled.

Chemeketa Community College
4000 Lancaster Drive, NE
PO Box 14007
Salem, OR 97309-7070
Ph: 503/399-5000
www.chemeketa.edu
President: Gerard I. Berger

Contacts

Wynn Cudmore, Principal Investigator
Chemeketa Community College
Ph: 503/399-6514
Fax: 503/589-7622
E-mail: wync@chemeketa.edu

Arthur McKee, Co-principal Investigator
Oregon State University
Ph: 541/750-7350
Fax: 541/750-7329
E-mail: mckee@FSL.orst.edu

Susie Kelly, Project Director
Chemeketa Community College
Ph: 503/315-4583
Fax: 503/589-7622
E-mail: kels@chemeketa.edu

Program Web Address
www.ncsr.org

You have rocked my world! I will never look at the discipline of biology in the same way again!
—*Community college participant at faculty development institute*

Program Profile

The Pacific Northwest, like other parts of the nation and world, faces major challenges in sustaining environments and economies and in developing education programs to meet present and emerging needs. In order to compete in a global economy, the nation's natural resource based agencies and industries are pressed to transform to a technological high-performance workplace. To meet these challenges, the Northwest Center for Sustainable Resources (NCSR) spearheads applications of new scientific and technological knowledge in secondary and community college education in natural resources programs. NCSR graduates receive technical degrees with advanced skills for the technological workforce, or they transfer to four-year colleges and universities to continue their education. Established on September 1, 1995, NCSR is a national collaboration of partners from education, business and industry, and other sectors. The center also manages an information network on related issues for the region and the nation.

Led by the center, 10 community colleges are developing and testing curricula for more than 50

Faculty "harness up" while attending a field tour to a world-renowned research site, the Wind River Canopy Crane Research Facility, in Wind River, Washington.

courses to be delivered in the coming years. Courses will be posted on the center's Web site. Week-long summer institutes—Ecosystem Institute, Natural Resource Institute, and GIS (geographic information systems) Institute—provide continuing education for high school teachers and community college faculty.

Underpinning the project's curriculum development activities are the core principles of ecosystem management, a relatively new approach to natural resource management. With ecosystem science at the core of ecosystem management, the principles include:

- maintaining existing biodiversity at genetic, species, and ecosystems levels
- maintaining evolutionary and ecological processes within ecosystems
- managing over temporal and spatial scales that are appropriate for the ecosystem
- maintaining long-term site productivity
- accommodating human uses within these constraints

With those principles in mind, NCSR has developed far-reaching objectives. First, it created a coordinated educational plan among secondary schools, community colleges, and four-year colleges and universities. With the goal of producing graduates with associate degrees and advanced degrees who will support the regional and global environment, the center is developing curricula in five resource management areas for two-year technician programs. Programs reflect emerging concepts of sustainability, ecosystem management, and other scientifically based concepts, as well as industry standards and public policies to restore and sustain natural resources. Innovative program models and courses are transportable and will be available as written materials and through the Web site. A clearinghouse and network would continue collaboration among partners. Dissemination of curricula is being accomplished through faculty development opportunities for community college and secondary educators, conferences and workshops, and the Web site. Other dissemination activities and visits help other regions of the country develop similar programs. The center's overall goal, through the use of these education models, is to strengthen natural resource technician programs throughout the nation and thereby help transform the American workplace to one of high performance.

Why This Approach?

The need for technicians educated in ecosystems-based natural resource management is substantiated in a number of ways. A study of entry-level professionals in forestry, reported in the *Journal of Forestry*, revealed that over the previous two years, employers had hired more than 1,100 foresters, nearly half of them for entry-level positions. Most positions were in state or local government. Others were in consulting firms, the federal government, or private industry. About 75 percent of these entry-level positions were filled at the bachelor's degree level, 18 percent at the associate degree level, and 2.4 percent at the master's degree level. However, employers filled close to 400 additional entry-level positions with applicants with a biological or environmental science background, despite the fact that about half of these jobs were primarily forestry positions. Eighteen percent of these employers said they deliberately had shifted hiring requirements from a forestry degree to a biological science degree to obtain employees with a broader science background.

The move toward more biologically educated natural resource technicians is a direct result of the increasing use of ecosystem-based management. It has been adopted by all federal land-management agencies and many state agencies. Companies such as Boise Cascade are developing demonstration sites (NCSR Visions report, p. 27). Thus, these new approaches to management form the underpinnings for the center's model. These approaches are being imbedded in NCSR's instructional design, and faculty from high school through university level are participating in NCSR institutes to learn these new ideas.

Partners

NCSR's success to date is largely attributable to the development of unique partnerships. The center works with a variety of organizations.

Lead community colleges. Central Oregon Community College, Oregon; Chemeketa Community College, Oregon; Feather River College, California; Grays Harbor College, Washington; and Shasta College, California.

Test site community colleges. Allegany College, Maryland; Blue Mountain Community College, Oregon; Everett Community College, Washington; Itasca Community College, Minnesota; and Mount Hood Community College, Oregon.

Other community colleges. Blackfeet Community College, Montana; Hawaii Community College; Haywood Community College, North Carolina; Northwest Indian College, Washington.

Employers and professional societies. Pacific Meridian Resources, Inc., Oregon; International Resources Unlimited, Inc., Oregon; Pacific Farms, California; Bureau of Land Management, Oregon; Sierra Pacific Industries, California; U.S. Forest Service, Tahoe National Forest, Nevada; Weyerhaeuser Company, Arkansas; Society of American Foresters, American Fisheries Society, and North American Wildlife Technology Association.

Native American groups. Through its Native American advisor, who is associated with the Confederated Tribes of the Siletz Indians, the center builds the needs and interests of various tribes into the program.

Research/university groups. H. J. Andrews Experimental Forest, Willamette National Forest, Oregon; Department of Forest Science, Oregon State University, Corvallis; Wind River Canopy Crane Research Facility, Washington. In addition to involving scientists and field sites in the center's institutes, research partners offer findings on aquatic and terrestrial ecosystems and advice in curriculum development.

High schools. Envirothon, known as the "environmental olympics," is the result of a collaboration among a variety of partners, particularly North Salem High School, Oregon Department of Education, Oregon Department of Fish and Wildlife, Governor's Watershed Enhancement Board, Oregon State University, and the Bureau of Land Management.

MAJOR ACHIEVEMENTS

Wide-ranging partnerships. Established and expanded various partnerships among educators, Native American tribes, research groups, and professional societies.

Curriculum. Revised, developed, and tested curricula in five natural resource based technical programs.

Continuing education. Offered faculty development institutes to high school, community college, and four-year college instructors from around the nation.

Information referral. Developing an electronic clearinghouse.

Visionary reports. Published and presented information on the program, including the center's interim report, *Visions for Natural Resource Education and Ecosystem Science for the 21st Century,* in state, regional, and national settings.

Tribal outreach. Organized outreach to Native American tribes, including hosting a tribal forum at Kah-Nee-Ta Resort on the Warm Springs Reservation in central Oregon and sponsoring annual Salmon Corps conferences. Published an interim report, *American Indian Perspectives: Nature, Natural Resources, and Natural Resources Education.* Native American perspectives are being incorporated into the center's courses.

High school activities. Hosted the annual Envirothon, known as an "environmental olympics."

Key collaborations. Established and expanded close working relationships with H. J. Andrews Experimental Forest, a NSF-funded long-term ecological research site, and other similar sites. Worked with various professional societies, including the Society of American Foresters and the North American Wildlife Technology Association, in program development, improvement, and certification.

The contact and conversations I had with colleagues from throughout the Northwest led to stimulating conversations and insights to other programs. These exchanges have continued. I see the institute having a long-range, positive impact on our program and on the 100 students that attend the program each year.
—*Community college participant at faculty development institute*

Influences on Program Development

Chemeketa Community College used a variety of outside resources to design the center's work. National Science Foundation guidelines served as a baseline, supplemented by the Secretary's Commission on Achieving Necessary Skills (SCANS) and the Developing a Curriculum (DACUM) process. College staff collaborated with other ATE projects and centers, including the Center for Image Processing in Education and the Advanced Technology Environmental Education Center/Partnership for Environmental Technology Education.

Partners have played key roles. Private industry, government agencies, and professional society members serve on the center's advisory committees, participate in faculty institutes, develop model student projects, and provide focus group interviews. They identify and develop field sites and also help develop or validate curricula through participation in DACUM design panels.

Student Recruitment

NCSR wants to attract as many students as it can to the environmental field in as many ways as it can. Staff connect with secondary schools in a variety of ways, including making classroom presentations and leading field labs. They participate in the annual Forest Field Days, a middle school and high school experience supported by the Oregon Forest Research Institute, and the annual two-day Fire School, a hands-on program to help high school students learn about forest fire control and use. Exhibits and presentations at the college's annual Career Expo and high school Career Days heighten student awareness of opportunities. A snappy program brochure provides details. Center staff also worked closely with officials responsible for developing Oregon's new Certificate of Advanced Mastery (CAM) in natural resources and with high school teachers involved in the CAM/AD associate degree project.

Lead colleges use additional recruitment approaches. Shasta College's agriculture technology program hosts students of all ages for various campus events and for field-based activities at its model farm facility. The college developed a model agreement with area high schools, the Eight Component Articulation Agreement. Feather River College developed a new articulation process called Highway to Success. Grays Harbor College and Chemeketa are working to recruit disadvantaged Native American young people who are members of the Salmon Corps.

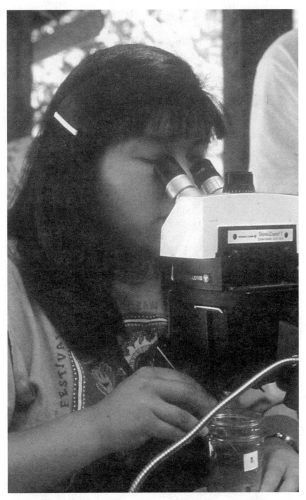

A community college faculty member examines invertebrate samples under a microscope during the Ecosystem Institute at the H. J. Andrews Experimental Forest, Blue River, Oregon.

The Natural Resources Institute experience proved to be a critical turning point for me in the way that I educate my students about our resources and their sustainability.
        —High school teacher at a faculty development institute

Unexpected Outcomes

Perhaps the most satisfying outcome is the sincere and heartfelt testimonials that partners have given the center. Staff members commonly hear that they are "doing a good thing—and the right thing." Interest from individuals and institutions around the nation exceeded expectations. Chemeketa Community College benefited from the development of the Aquatic Ecology Laboratory, the expansion of the forest resource technology program, and the establishment of new partnerships with state and local agencies and businesses that have provided new opportunities for students.

Center staff report that the secondary education component of the center's work is much richer than originally envisioned. The evidence is clear—collaborative efforts with the Environmental Education Association of Oregon, the statewide Envirothon, tours of the Wind River Canopy Crane Research Facility, presentations at annual meetings of the National Science Teachers' Association and National Association of Biology Teachers, and numerous other events. Another significant outcome is the number of positive relationships between various education components that can facilitate innovation in science education.

Natural resource management is not just about cutting trees anymore. We are stewards of the earth. We need to take greater pride in what we do. The community college is an excellent way to filter in old folks like myself.
        —Older student employed for years by a traditional timber company

The Natural Resources Institute experience proved to be a critical turning point for me in the way that I educate my students about our resources and their sustainability.

—High school teacher at a faculty development institute

Technical and academic faculty.
Technical and academic faculty at community colleges traditionally have operated in two different worlds. Administrative structures often promote this separation and the groups' paths cross only occasionally. As a result of more math and science courses being infused into NCSR curriculum and the incorporation of these skills into technical curriculum, technical faculty now call upon their colleagues across campus to develop and revise curricula for their technical programs. Conversely, science and math faculty and their students benefit by becoming more aware of practical applications of their disciplines.

Community colleges. Community colleges often are isolated from one another. The NCSR partnership involves a cooperating network of community colleges that develops, revises, and tests natural resources curricula. Course content, teaching strategies, contacts, funding sources, and other elements of curriculum improvement are regularly exchanged at periodic meetings, NCSR institutes, and informal gatherings. The project's model of curriculum development, implementation, and testing at lead sites, followed by adaptation, review, and implementation at test sites, fosters a working relationship between the colleges. Such relationships did not exist prior to NCSR.

Universities and community colleges.
Universities often view community colleges as stepchildren of the higher education system. NCSR's activities have changed this perception. Every NCSR lead institution developed a formal articulation agreement with at least one, and sometimes several, universities. The agreements require close examination of course syllabi and materials, a process that has given universities a better appreciation of the quality of work performed at community colleges and community colleges a greater understanding of how to better prepare students for transfer into baccalaureate programs.

Community colleges and high schools.
Each NCSR lead college developed or strengthened relationships with its district high schools. The relationships provide mutual benefits. For the community college, student recruitment for technical programs increases. For the high school, additional resources in the form of community college expertise and materials become available to them.

High schools and their communities.
NCSR secondary programs foster partnerships among secondary schools, agencies, industries, higher education, and communities. The center provides teachers with experiences to develop a new model for education in which students become active, participatory citizens who use science to solve community problems. Since ecosystem management hinges on interactions among social, economic, and ecological components of natural resources to achieve "true sustainability," partnerships with the community, public agencies, and the private sector undergird the secondary program effort.

Community colleges and employers.
Although all NCSR programs have had working relationships with employers, these

As President/CEO of International Resources Unlimited, Inc., I have had many opportunities to talk with others about this unique program. Those I have spoken with have expressed great interest in, and admiration for, the efforts of NCSR. Congratulations on a well-run program.

—Corporate partner

relationships have expanded as a result of the center's efforts. For example, the center has convened representatives from federal and state agencies and private industry to assist educators in each curriculum to define tasks required for specific jobs in natural resources. Each program has used the DACUM process prior to curriculum development. Additionally, employers have opened up the lands they manage as field sites for students. Employers have looked to NCSR as a resource to establish partnerships with other elements of education. In addition, partner community colleges provide student internships and continuing education opportunities for employees.

Other positive relationships include partners from the center's national visiting committee and advisory committee who have helped the center create opportunities by linking college faculty with leading industries and world-renowned research sites, among others. Leading scientists and agency and industry personnel have partnered with the center to make presentations at the Ecosystem Institute and Natural Resource Institute. Those partners include researchers from the H. J.

There is no doubt that I am now much better equipped to carry out my administrative and professional duties [as the result of participation in the GIS Institute]. I must say that it was one of the most enjoyable educational experiences in the past 20 years.

—State government official who participated in a faculty development institute

Andrews Experimental Forest and representatives from the Oregon Department of Fish and Wildlife, the Bureau of Land Management, the U.S. Forest Service, and GIS firms.

Central to the program's operation are the relationships between NCSR and the 10 lead and test community colleges, which revise and test courses and programs, produce national products, and shepherd interaction with high schools and four-year colleges and universities. Their distinctive roles are shown below.

Lead College	Curriculum	Test Site
Central Oregon Community College, Bend, Oregon	Forestry/Eastside and Geographic Information Systems (GIS) Technology	Allegany College, Cumberland, Maryland
Chemeketa Community College, Salem, Oregon	Environmental Science (core curriculum)	Everett Community College, Everett, Washington
Chemeketa Community College, Salem, Oregon	Forestry/Westside Technology	Allegany College, Cumberland, Maryland
Feather River College, Quincy, California	Wildlife Technology	Itasca Community College, Grand Rapids, Minnesota
Grays Harbor College, Aberdeen, Washington	Fisheries/Natural Resources Technology	Mount Hood Community College, Gresham, Oregon
Shasta College Redding, California	Agriculture Technology	Blue Mountain Community College, Pendleton, Oregon

I can't believe we did this. It is sooo cool!
—*Student in the Edge Effect Lab, an environmental science field laboratory*

Recognition

In its first five years, the Northwest Center for Sustainable Resources has showcased its program at conferences and symposia in more than 30 settings. It also received a number of awards and notices during this period. Twice, Chemeketa Community College's forest resource technology program was awarded a Certificate of Environmental Achievement, and the program has appeared in Renew America's *Environmental Success Index* of 1997 and 1998. This award signifies that the program has successfully undergone a rigorous verification process, including local and state evaluation and careful screening by the National Awards Council for Environmental Sustainability. An article in *Forestry Source*, a national publication produced by the 18,000-member Society of American Foresters, featured NCSR. The NCSR secondary education coordinator was elected president of the Environmental Education Association of Oregon, the state chapter of the North American Association for Environmental Education.

Feather River College's wildlife and fisheries program received full accreditation (for three years) from the North American Wildlife Technology Association. This is the only accredited wildlife program in the western United States. Grays Harbor College's fisheries technology program developed an articulation agreement with the University of Washington's School of Fisheries—a major success following years of effort. This model agreement enables associate degree students to transfer approximately 75 percent of their courses to the university, some of them counting for upper-level credit at the university.

Student achievement has been rewarded with academic scholarships. Chemeketa students have received Oregon Logging Conference, Vista Masonic, and Valsetz scholarships. Shasta College students have received scholarships from the Shasta County Cattlemen's Association and the Shasta Rose Society.

Central Oregon Community College's forest technology program continues to be recognized through the Society of American Foresters, among about only 20 other programs nationwide. Recognition affirms that the program has exemplary staff and rigorous curricula based on national standards. Shasta College's agriculture and natural resources technology program received a public service award from the Sacramento Coordinated Water Quality and Monitoring Program through the Whiskeytown National Recreation Area.

College Commitment

Much of NCSR's success to date is due to the commitment and participation by Chemeketa's board of education and college administrators and staff. Dedicated personnel combined with a fine facility and a state-of-the-art information technology department provide the backbone for the center model. Key commitments come from the college's dean of campus-based instruction, who serves as fiscal manager, and the college's president and vice president, who maintain formal and informal connections with the project. The campus community provides numerous support staff from departments, including contracts, business, media/graphics, information technology, and others. Chemeketa's forest resource technology program and the environmental science program are supported both by administrative personnel and with the use of

Students in Chemeketa's environmental science class take initial measurements on logs which will be part of a 20-year study on log decomposition.

I have been given a rock-solid foundation for continuing my education and career in environmental science.
—Community college student

campus field sites. For example, the college committed funds and an expansive field site to develop the new Aquatic Ecology Laboratory.

Leveraged Funds

NCSR's grant from the National Science Foundation leveraged sizable support in the form of equipment and software for curriculum development and for improving field sites. Chemeketa's Aquatic Ecology Laboratory leveraged $120,000 for the field site, stockwater tanks, and equipment, including sensors and computer-based technologies. At Feather River College, GIS software donations from the Environmental Systems Research Institute totaled $75,000. Central Oregon Community College received another $100,000. A research vessel and GIS software and hardware valued at $150,000 were given to Grays Harbor College. Shasta College's donations include agricultural equipment worth $150,000.

What's Next?

NCSR's fundamental work is changing the way natural resource education is conducted. Changing "traditional dogmas" and producing real and lasting changes require significant and sustained efforts. Making change permanent requires creating and promoting exceptional products. For these reasons, among others, NCSR places high priority on sustaining activities beyond the advanced technological education grant funding, which will be completed in 2001. Adaptation and implementation of materials by other programs throughout the nation will be a primary goal for the center in the future.

The center will seek renewal funding through NSF so it can continue to serve as a focal point for natural resource technology. Institutes may be supported through fees or through private funding, and the institutes themselves may be expanded. For example, the high school Natural Resource Institute may serve as Oregon's outstanding information resource for education reform. As a result

of the Oregon Education Reform Act, which mandated the development of a Natural Resource Certificate of Advanced Mastery (CAM), NCSR can lead the effort to provide in-service faculty training opportunities for schools and districts across the state. The principles of sustainability through ecosystem-based management, delivered with a community-based approach, will continue the mission and philosophy of the Natural Resource Institute.

NCSR will continue to produce curriculum-based materials in multimedia and print formats. Web-based and written materials will be available for multiple educational levels. Capitalizing on the popularity of, and need for, GIS materials and support, NCSR will increase activities in this area. It will produce additional institutes and materials suitable for secondary and community college programs.

To meet these goals, NCSR is increasing its outreach and impact through marketing, newsletters, conference presentations, international collaboration, and continued and new partnerships. NCSR partners can contribute materials to the clearinghouse, link to the NCSR Web site, and get information on curricula, training, internships, and jobs.

Materials Produced by the Program

NCSR course and other materials are available for free from the center.

Curriculum Materials

Fisheries and Wildlife Technology
Introduction to Wildlife
Fish and Game Laws
Introduction to Fish, Amphibians, and Reptiles
Introduction to Mammals
Ornithology
Introduction to Fisheries Management
Introduction to Aquaculture
Advanced Aquaculture
Fisheries Biology
Wildlife Management
Watershed Ecosystems: Functions, Monitoring

Core Courses
Environmental Science I, II, III

Support Courses
    Wildlife Conservation
    Introduction to Natural Resources
    Introduction to Chemistry
    Soils
    Technical Mathematics
    Environmental Ethics
    Range Ecosystem Management
    Ecosystem Inventory and Measurement
    Resource Economics
    Computers in Environmental Resources
    Chemistry Applied to the Environment
    Ecology
    Chemical and Biological Field
       and Lab Methods
    Society and Forestry

Forest Resources Technology
    Introduction to Forest Survey
    Aerial Photo Interpretation
    Forest Ecology
    Resource Measurements
    Forest Stand Dynamics
    Resource Sampling
    Wildlife Ecology
    Silvicultural Methods
    Forest Inventory
    Forest Insect and Disease
    Forest Policy
    Forest Management Problem Solving
    Forest Practices for Ecosystem Management

Agriculture Technology
    Agriculture Records and Analysis
    Plant Science
    Mechanical Technology
    Holistic Management
    Principles of Animal Science
    Agriculture and Natural Resource Practices

Geographic Information Systems (GIS)
    Introduction to GIS
    GIS Dataset Creation
    Remote Sensing
    Data Conversion and Documentation
    ArcInfo

Informational Publications

American Indian perspectives: Nature, natural resources, and natural resources education. 1999. 130 pages.

Employers in natural resources: What they're telling us. 1998. 46 pages.

Native American perspectives in natural resources and environmental technology. 1998. Proceedings of the NCSR Tribal Forum, July. 44-page report and eight-minute videotape.

Northwest Center for Sustainable Resources. 1999. Education for a sustainable future. 13-minute videotape.

Visions for natural resource education and ecosystem science for the 21st century. 1998. An Interim Report of the Northwest Center for Sustainable Resources, March. 126 pages.

References

Brown, T. L., and J. P. Lassoie. 1998. *Entry-level competency and skill requirements of foresters.* Journal of Forestry, 96(2): 8-14.

Northwest Center for Sustainable Resources. 1998. *Visions for natural resource education and ecosystem science for the 21st century: interim report.* Salem, Ore.: Northwest Center for Sustainable Resources.

Bellevue Community College
Bellevue, Washington

NorthWest Center for Emerging Technologies (NWCET)

► **FOCUS**
► Information technology (IT) skill standards
► Standards-based curriculum products and services
► Faculty development
► Student pathways to IT programs and degrees

College Environment

Established in 1966, Bellevue Community College in Bellevue, Washington, serves King County, on the western side of the Cascade Mountains in the heart of the "silicon forest." The county's population grew 9 percent between 1990 and 1997. The college's service area includes incorporated cities and towns, unincorporated communities, and six school districts. More ethnically and racially diverse than the state as a whole, King County is 82.2 percent white, 5.1 percent African American, 1.2 percent Native American, and 8.0 percent Asian. The county has the highest median income in the state, with a median household income of $53,000. There have been steady but gradual increases in the numbers of high school graduates in the service area.

The college offers two-year associate degrees, certificate programs, continuing education options, and preparation programs to begin a four-year degree. The student population numbers about 19,000. Sixty-two percent of the college's overall population is female; 60 percent of its credit population is 25 years of age or younger. The college's curricula include 63 degrees and programs, and its job placement rate averages 77 percent.

Bellevue Community College
3000 Landerholm Circle, SE
Bellevue, Washington 98007-6484
Ph: 425/564-1000
www.bcc.ctc.edu
President: B. Jean Floten

Contacts
Neil Evans, Principal Investigator
Executive Director
NorthWest Center for Emerging Technologies
Ph: 425/564-4227
Fax: 425/564-6193
E-mail: nevans@bcc.ctc.edu

Peter Saflund, Co-principal Investigator
Associate Director
NorthWest Center for Emerging Technologies
Ph: 425/564-4216
Fax: 425/564-6193
E-mail: psaflund@bcc.ctc.edu

Program Web Address
www.nwcet.org

Program Profile

NWCET designed a variety of activities to support new and innovative information technology (IT) programs and degrees. Heading the list is an extensive

Establishing industry-based skill standards is essential: to ensure that employers understand what knowledge and skills are needed for present and future success; to focus the attention of educators and corporate training organizations on industry requirements; and to signal to students and employees what knowledge, skills, and abilities will be valued and rewarded in the workplace.

—*Corporate executive*

portfolio of electronic courseware, curriculum development kits, teaching and learning packets, online resources, and other products based on NWCET's skill standards for information technology.

In a cooperative venture between education and business, NWCET developed skill standards for the IT field, which faces a serious skills gap in its workforce. Approximately 200 IT professionals in regional and national companies worked together to generate data that comprise skill standards in eight clusters. The Washington State Board of Community and Technical Colleges provided funds to help identify IT skill standards. Colleges across the country are adopting the skill standards, designed specifically to enhance education methodologies, for use in IT certificate and degree programs. The standards, all nationally validated, appear in a book profiling emerging IT careers, the millennium edition of *Building a Foundation for Tomorrow: Skill Standards for Information Technology*. NWCET and Bellevue launched the successful first edition of the book in 1997.

NWCET provides professional development opportunities for high school teachers and community college, four-year college, and university faculty. For example, the center's Educator to Educator (E2E) program was launched in early 2000 to provide instructor training in areas such as e-commerce, database management, and network administration.

In order to encourage students to attain a bachelor's degree, NWCET works with an extensive partnership network to help structure transfer agreements among participating institutions. The agreements provide community college students with opportunities for seamless transfer to four-year programs and ensure consistency in the catalog of standards applicable to a variety of IT degree programs.

By developing and disseminating information about IT careers, NWCET actively recruits students for such careers, with a special focus on increasing the diversity of the IT workforce.

NWCET strives to meet the needs of employers and educators through strong partnerships with government, industry, and educational institutions. Its research and development efforts in IT education, professional development programs, and student recruitment and retention programs substantiate its leadership role in the field. The National Science Foundation first funded NWCET in 1995 and added funding through a renewal grant in 1998. Significant additional financial support has come from Seattle-based companies such as the Microsoft Corporation and the Boeing Company, as well as from the Washington State Board for Community and Technical Colleges.

Project partners have played a vital role in NWCET's success. Microsoft and Boeing, in particular, not only contributed significant funds for construction of the center itself, but also continue to make available corporate staff to serve as consultants and members of active advisory committees. In addition to an ATE grant, Bellevue won support from the National Science Foundation for supplemental projects, including the National Validation

The NWCET facility.

of Skill Standards, NWCET IT Curriculum Adaptation and Implementation, and Cyber Careers for the Net Generation.

Why This Approach?

Extensive research has revealed a severe lack of qualified employees in the field of information technology. This problem is further intensified by a lack of consistency in identified skill standards on which to base educational programs and a failure to provide comprehensive advanced technology education that includes extensive technical skills supported by strong foundation skills.

The Northwest Center for Emerging Technologies (NWCET)—through partnerships with a number of information technology leaders representing corporations, professional organizations, and educational institutions—has taken a leadership role in determining the needs of IT employees and prospective students. In this role, the NWCET has identified IT skill standards and has used them to develop competency-based curricula for IT students.

Influences on Program Development

As one of the first recipients of a National Science Foundation grant to develop an advanced technological education center, Bellevue was a pioneer of sorts. The NWCET program was heavily influenced by the needs and views of the IT industry in Washington State and elsewhere.

Student Recruitment

NWCET undertook several projects to engage women and minorities more actively in the IT field. While IT traditionally has not been the first career choice for these groups, NWCET staff advocates new approaches to help change perspectives and provide new opportunities. Two examples of the center's recruitment and retention efforts are the IT All Stars and the Cyber Careers for the Net Generation projects.

IT All Stars—Building Bridges Today for Success Tomorrow: A Youth Information Technology Showcase. IT All Stars is a team-based competition to create an IT product. It is open to middle and high school students in Washington State's King and Pierce Counties. Finalists showcase their IT products at the NWCET facility. The center collaborates with

PARTNERS

Microsoft Corporation. Provided and continues to provide major strategic input and funding, including $1,000,000 in cash and in-kind support to NWCET projects such as the Summer Institute, an IT recruitment video, and the Youth Information Technology All-Stars Showcase.

The Boeing Company. Provided and continues to provide major strategic input and funding, including $1,000,000 for construction of the NWCET building and cash and in-kind support to NWCET projects such as scholarships, online course development, and development kits for the information technology curriculum.

Harcourt College Publishers. Co-developing with NWCET a series of online courses that will lead to certificate programs in Web authoring as well as certificate and associate degree programs in computer information systems and networking—all based on the NWCET skill standard–based curricula. Courses will include state-of-the-art graphics, animation, simulations, and technical and pedagogical design.

American Electronics Association. Collaborated on the national validation and update of skill standards, contributed $20,000, and helped organize national industry-expert review and update panels.

The Chauncey Group International. Developing vendor-neutral, nationally applicable assessment instruments and related materials for use in academic, educational, and scholastic markets.

Education Development Center. Partnering in implementing NWCET-developed model curricula, skill standards, and best practices for high school IT Tech Prep programs and community college IT programs and courses.

Western Governors University. Collaborating on the development of online courseware for IT course and program offerings based on NWCET's

continued on next page…

...continued

skill standards. Bellevue Community College provides degrees and certificates through the WGU distance learning program.

American Association of Community Colleges. Serves as the educational and academic distributor of the millennium edition of *Building a Foundation for Tomorrow: Skill Standards for Information Technology.*

University of Phoenix. Strategic partner in the development and maintenance of information technology skill standards. The university will develop or derive its curricula, courseware, and training materials from NWCET's *Skill Standards.*

Gartner Institute. Business partnership to financially support the NWCET annual research and update of NWCET's *Skill Standards*, and to develop, publish, market and distribute corporate and individual training based on *Skill Standards.*

Institute of Electrical and Electronics Engineers, Inc. Partnership to design and develop Cyber Careers for the Net Generation (a suite of materials including video, Web site, and print materials), which will introduce students to the vast number of careers available in the field of IT and a glimpse into these jobs.

OTHER PARTNERS

Business. Digital Creators, NetG, Society for Information Management, and Washington Software Alliance.

Education. Colorado Electronic Community College, EDUCAUSE, Florida Community College Distance Learning Consortium, Maryland Department of Education, Regional Advanced Technology Education Consortium, University of Washington, and Washington State Board for Community and Technical Colleges.

Government. U.S. Department of Commerce, U.S. Department of Education, U.S. Department of Labor, and Northwest Regional Educational Laboratory.

the Women's Community Impact Consortium, a community-based nonprofit organization dedicated to providing technology skills to minority women and children. Local IT professionals mentor the teams. The Technology Access Foundation, a group committed to bringing technology to communities of color, provided three state-of-the-art multimedia stations as prizes for the competition. The event is held concurrently with the American Association of University Women's Expanding Your Horizons program, which provides information and activities to attract middle school girls to science careers. Students attending Expanding Your Horizons are invited to attend the showcase and keynotes.

Cyber Careers for the Net Generation. NWCET and the Educational Activities Department of the Institute of Electrical and Electronics Engineers (IEEE) collaborate on the development of a suite of IT career education materials including a video, a Web site, and print materials. This product provides outreach to several audiences, including women and minorities, teachers, counselors, and middle and high school students. The central purpose is to inform students about IT careers and to attract underrepresented populations to the IT profession. The focus is on the dual goals of emphasizing the appeal of the profession for younger students (middle and high school students) and projecting a positive image of the IT worker.

In addition to these projects, NWCET offers a variety of other recruitment efforts that reach out to high school students. Tech Days is an event that introduces students from area high schools to the IT field and careers by bringing them to the Bellevue Community College campus to attend hands-on workshops and IT professional panels. NWCET staff are frequently asked to provide information sessions on IT careers at western Washington-area high schools and to participate in high school career days. Members of the staff also made presentations at Microsoft Corporation's 1999 Diversity Day.

Because of the nationally recognized work NWCET has done on the IT career clusters and their collaboration with industry and academic institutions throughout the country, we know they'll ensure thorough development of skill standards for emerging IT career clusters.

—Corporate training leader

Unexpected Outcomes

Bellevue Community College found a greater-than-anticipated thirst on the part of faculty, government, and industry representatives for definitive information on IT skill standards, their relevance to employment, and their benefit to students. As a result of early success with the IT skills standards, the college was selected in 1998 as a mentor college in Working Connections, a national initiative co-sponsored by the Microsoft Corporation and the American Association of Community Colleges. As a Working Connections mentor college, Bellevue and NWCET staffs provide technical assistance to other community colleges across the country.

That same year, the U. S. Department of Commerce chose Bellevue Community College and NWCET to host a national town meeting addressing the IT worker shortage. A few months later, in January 1999, the college and NWCET were invited to be one of only 12 colleges nationwide to participate in Vice President Al Gore's National Summit on 21st Century Skills for 21st Century Jobs. Held in Washington, D.C., the forum focused on IT jobs and skills.

Due in part to NWCET's accomplishments, Bellevue Community College won a $750,000 demonstration grant from the U.S. Department of Labor to train displaced workers—including women, minorities, and people over 40 years of age—in IT careers. The college was one of only 11 in the nation to win this grant. Bellevue partners with its local private industry council in this project to provide education and training in network support, technical support, programming, and online technical writing. Two students in the first graduating class landed jobs with annual salaries of $75,000.

Recognition

NWCET senior staff serve on the advisory boards of a number of prestigious organizations, including the National Academy of Sciences, Gartner Institute, Washington State Skill Standards Implementation Committee, and Microsoft's Skills

MAJOR ACHIEVEMENTS

IT skill standards. Developed and published an IT skill standards document—Building a Foundation for Tomorrow: Information Technology Skill Standards—and distributed it to more than 5,000 community college faculty and industry training centers.

IT skill standards-based curriculum kit. Developed and published a standards-based curriculum development kit to help instructors build new programs.

IT Tech Prep. Developed and implemented a high school IT Tech Prep curriculum.

Transfer agreements. Established seamless transfer agreements between nine western Washington community colleges and the newly established bachelor of science degree program in computing and software systems at the University of Washington, Bothell.

Conferences. Sponsored and collaborated on a number of conferences, including: Edu.Tech@Work-96 and Edu.Tech@Work-97, two national conferences that drew nearly 800 participants and fostered communication between business leaders and educators; Work Now and in the Future 15 (1998), a regional conference cosponsored with the Northwest Regional Educational Laboratory, which attracted nearly 2,000 educators, business people, workforce developers, and trainers.

Dissemination of best practices. Conducted the first National Science Foundation Advanced Technology Centers Best Practices Workshop to discuss common issues and lay the groundwork for developing an ATE information network and an ATE forum on the NWCET Web site.

2000 Advisory Council. A number of other examples illustrate the recognition that the ATE center has earned.

NWCET has received important recognition at the federal level. The Department of Commerce invited Bellevue president Jean Floten to be one of four panelists at a June 1998 meeting at the National Press Club in Washington, D.C., to unveil the report that came out of a successful year-long series of town meetings on IT worker shortage.

Organizers of the vice president's National Summit invited an information technology graduate from Bellevue and the executive director of NWCET to attend the prestigious event.

NWCET has formed positive connections with the Microsoft Corporation. Microsoft profiled NWCET in a video case study in April 1999 and made the study available on the Microsoft Web site. Later that summer, Bellevue, NWCET, Microsoft, and the Washington State Board for Community and Technical Colleges co-produced the first Microsoft IT Educator's Summer Institute. This is a week-long summer institute for Washington State community college IT faculty to upgrade their skills and help them develop new

skill standards-based curricula. The program was revised and provided again in summer 2000 and also adapted to train faculty in the Working Connections program co-sponsored by Microsoft and the American Association of Community Colleges. As a Working Connections mentor college, Bellevue is a national leader for IT curriculum development in other community colleges across the country. Bellevue also has won or been responsible for generating approximately 80 faculty industry fellowships with Microsoft.

NWCET has made a mark internationally as well. Microsoft and the European Union (EU) asked NWCET to consult on the development of skill standards in the EU to close the technology gap in Europe. NWCET's IT skill standards were used as an international model. NWCET staff also attended the US-Euro-net IT skills meeting in Washington, D.C. In North America, NWCET is advising the Canadian Software Human Resources Council and National Research Council of Canada on IT workforce solutions.

Several groups are using the IT skill standards set out by NWCET:

- IEEE published portions of *Building a Foundation for Tomorrow: Skill Standards for Information Technology* in a CD ROM titled *Careers for Electrical and Computer Scientists.*
- The American Electronics Association and Western Governors University have adopted the IT skill standards.
  - The Washington Software and Digital Media Alliance (now Washington Software Alliance) endorsed NWCET's skill standards.
  - NWCET offers assistance to the National Skill Standards Board in the use and application of IT skill standards and provides information on the general nature and scope of IT careers.
  - The Washington State Board of Community and Technical Colleges awarded the center a workforce training pilot grant to implement IT skill standards in a program in technical support at Bellevue Community College.

The center is a member of the Seattle Technology Challenge Grant Consortium and will collaborate as such to build skill

Morgan Davis and Neil Evans at Vice President Al Gore's National IT Summit in Washington, D.C.

Students want assurance that the training they are receiving is relevant and marketable. Skill standards provide a template for educators to consult in structuring courses and experiences that define the employable graduate.

— *Federal official*

standards-based curricula (with funds of approximately $7 million over five years).

Under the auspices of NWCET, occupational programming degrees from nine western Washington community colleges are now linked with a newly established bachelor of science degree program in computing and software systems at the University of Washington, Bothell. For the first time, this linkage offers an option for baccalaureate transfer for more than 2,000 IT students at these community colleges.

Since the beginning of the ATE grant, project staff have made presentations at more than 300 local, regional, and national meetings sponsored by government, professional societies, national education associations, and private industry, including the League for Innovation, American Association of Community Colleges, Work Now and in the Future, EDUCAUSE, Washington Software Alliance, Arizona Software Alliance, Information Technology Association of America, National Educational Computing Conference, Society for Information Management, Institute of Electrical and Electronics Engineers, National School-to-Work Convocation, TechEd, EdMedia, and numerous state-sponsored IT and technology education conferences.

These presentations, as well as the extraordinary financial support Bellevue Community College and NWCET have received (more than $11 million), are important indicators of the regard with which the college and center are held by business leaders, other educators, and professional and government organizations in the Pacific Northwest and nationally.

College Commitment

Bellevue Community College has provided strong, top-level administrative support to NWCET and

has committed significant financial and other institutional support as well. It serves as the center's fiscal agent and provides technical support through the electronic infrastructure, physical location, faculty collaborative assistance, printing, and maintenance and business services. Computer equipment supplied for the Faculty Resource Center includes computers, printers, and scanners. Lab directors and technical support assistants staff computer labs for students. Faculty not supported by grant funds contribute to NWCET projects such as the development of IT skill standards and training programs for other instructors. The Bellevue Community College bookstore disseminates NWCET products.

Leveraged Funds

NWCET has successfully generated a wealth of additional resources from several sources for its work. They include:

- American Association of Community Colleges and Microsoft—Working Connections Mentor College grant
- Asymetrix—Multimedia Toolbook Software Training grant
- Bellevue Community College Foundation—equipment and furniture for NWCET
- Bellevue Community College—Internet Web server and home page for dissemination of information, as well as the LAN infrastructure, network manager, and HelpDesk
- The Boeing Company—funds for the center facility, loaned executives, and a grant for printing and production of 5,000 IT skill standards documents; additionally, a grant for printing and production of 1,500 Development Kits for IT Curriculum, and partial funding for Tech Prep IT Curriculum Lesson Plans; and two Boeing IT program scholarships
- Microsoft Corporation—software and faculty industry fellowships as well as copies of Microsoft Certified Systems Engineer (MCSE) study materials and grants for three NWCET Summer Institutes
- IEEE—grant to support the development of Cyber Careers for the Net Generation
- Gartner Institute—grant to develop IT skill standards-based business derivatives
- US West—distance learning grant
- J3 Learning—50 copies of J3 Learning Software

I feel confident that my skills will keep me a valued commodity in the marketplace on into the next century.
                                        —*Student*

- Washington State Board for Community and Technical Colleges—grants for information technology standards, computer literacy and assessment, and accelerated tech support, and partial funding for NWCET Summer Institute
- Washington State Department of Archives—co-location at the center facility
- Washington State and Bellevue Community College—computer proficiency lab equipment
- Washington Software and Digital Media Alliance (now Washington Software Alliance)—grant for dissemination of NWCET's *Skill Standards*

What's Next?

NWCET's goal is to become self-sufficient by the end of the NSF funding period through a variety of strategic business partnerships. A marketing plan for its products and services is under development. Through partnerships with publishers such as Harcourt College Publishers, NWCET is collaborating on the creation of online curriculum materials based on IT skill standards that will be marketed for sale. Another partnership with Gartner Institute is developing business derivatives from the IT skill standards and will sell products in the business market. Work with the Education Development Center will create a series of professional development workshops for high school, two-year, and four-year college faculty.

Materials Produced by the Program

Building a Foundation for Tomorrow: A Development Kit for Skill Standards-based Information Technology Curriculum. 1998. Bellevue, Wash.: NorthWest Center for Emerging Technologies. Available from bookstore, Bellevue Community College, 3000 Landerholm Circle, S.E., Bellevue, WA 98007-6484. ($200 each, plus shipping and handling)

Building a Foundation for Tomorrow: Skill Standards for Information Technology. Millennium Edition. 1999. Bellevue, Wash.: NorthWest Center for Emerging Technologies. Available from Community College Press, P.O. Box 311, Annapolis, MD 20701-0311. (Order #8047, $75 AACC members, $100 nonmembers)

Building a Foundation for Tomorrow: Tech Prep Information Technology Skill Standards-based Curriculum Modules. 1997. 2 vols. Bellevue, Wash.: NorthWest Center for Emerging Technologies. Available from bookstore, Bellevue Community College, 3000 Landerholm Circle, S.E., Bellevue, WA 98007-6484. ($200 each, plus shipping and handling)

Sinclair Community College
Dayton, Ohio

National Center of Excellence for Advanced Manufacturing Education

► FOCUS
► Associate degree in manufacturing engineering technology
► Integrated, contextual learning
► Industry-verified competencies

College Environment

Sinclair Community College is located in the southwest part of Ohio, in Montgomery County, an area comprising approximately 225,000 households. Dayton is the primary municipality. Historically a blue-collar area dominated by manufacturing, the county today has a larger proportion of its jobs and services focused in the wholesale and retail sectors. With a population of a little more than half a million, and a median household income of $38,221, the college's service area is approximately 79 percent white and 20 percent African American.

The college is located in the center of downtown Dayton and serves more than 20,000 students. Established by the voters of the county, it is operated by the Montgomery County Community College District. Revenues are derived from tax levies approved by the voters of Montgomery County, the State of Ohio, and fees paid by students. It opened its doors in 1948 when its first classes were held in YMCA buildings. It emerged that year from the YMCA college that had offered night school classes since 1887. Sinclair Community College offers hundreds of credit and non-credit courses available at the downtown Dayton campus, 15 neighborhood centers, 23 senior center sites, and through distance learning.

Sinclair Community College
444 West Third Street
Dayton, Ohio 45402-1460
Ph: 937-512-2500
www.sinclair.edu
President: Ned Sifferlen

Contacts
Tony Polsinelli, Principal Investigator
Director
The Advanced Integrated Manufacturing Center
Ph: 937/512-2989
Fax: 937/512-5372
E-mail: tpolsine@sinclair.edu

Bonnie L. Coe, Co-principal Investigator
Project Manager
The Advanced Integrated Manufacturing Center
Ph: 937/512-2219
Fax: 937/512-2394
E-mail: bcoe@sinclair.edu

Program Web Address
www.aimcenter.org

Sinclair grants associate degrees in arts, sciences, applied science, and individualized and technical study. The Technology Accreditation Commission of the Accreditation Board for Engineering and Technology accredits programs in

[I liked] being presented with what seemed like something outrageously difficult and being able to decompose the problem into smaller workable problems. I like the integration of both using hardware and software to solve the problem.

—Pilot test student

mechanical engineering technology, quality engineering technology, packaging engineering technology, electronics engineering technology, and industrial engineering technology.

Sinclair's study body is 40 percent male and 60 percent female. One percent of the student population is below the age of 17, 15 percent are between 17 and 19 years of age, and 38 percent are between 20 and 29 years of age. Thirty percent of the students are between 30 to 49 years old, 10 percent are between 50 to 72, and 6 percent are over 72 years of age. Minorities comprise about one-fifth of the student body, most of those African American. Nearly three-quarters of all students pursue an associate degree in one of the six academic divisions at Sinclair, with 10 percent pursuing a degree in engineering technology.

Program Profile

The National Center of Excellence for Advanced Manufacturing Education (NCE/AME) is a national partnership focused on developing a customer-driven approach to manufacturing education. Funded in part by the National Science Foundation's Advanced Technological Education program, the center is an affiliate of the Advanced Integrated Manufacturing (AIM) Center, a partnership between Sinclair Community College and the University of Dayton. NCE/AME encourages strong customer/supplier relationships between manufacturers and educators. It has created a novel new competency-driven associate degree program in manufacturing engineering technology. It seeks to create supporting modularized materials to support the new associate degree program and is validating each module through application and

use in the existing associate degree manufacturing engineering technology program.

The purpose of the partnership is to develop a manufacturing engineering technician who will work as a key member of the team responsible for manufacturing products and systems within a manufacturing enterprise. The team participates in production planning and control, and in production operations, quality, manufacturing systems planning, and maintenance management. Particularly in some small- to medium-sized enterprises, an experienced technician may be given responsibility for some aspects of manufacturing operations. In any case, the technician interacts with the professionals in the company and may also have contact with customers.

Specifically, NCE/AME's primary goals are to:
- develop a new competency-based, occupationally verified, seamless curriculum beginning in grade 11, through the associate of applied science degree, culminating with the bachelor of science degree using advanced manufacturing as the focus; with gateways to and from industrial employment throughout
- write, pilot test, and publish curriculum materials (laboratory manuals, video, software, and other ancillary materials) to improve mathematics, science, and manufacturing engineering technology instruction
- disseminate the curriculum, curriculum materials, and model program nationally

The competency-based, occupationally verified approach ensures that the skills students acquire will enable them to become quick contributors to the companies that employ them as members of a production operations team. The college claims that the curriculum and supporting modularized curriculum material is "occupationally verified" because industry leaders and experts helped identify the competencies to be covered, participated in the development of the material, and reviewed the material before it was finalized and published. The curriculum materials emphasize hands-on activities throughout, enabling participants to build a strong foundation of analytical and problem-solving skills required for lifelong learning and technical growth. The curriculum includes an introductory "big picture" module, nine clusters of course modules, and a major capstone experience. All these parts are

I liked the math. I usually hate math, but I liked it when it was applied to something tangible.

—*Pilot test student*

coordinated with an integrating manufacturing experience. This is a learning activity that requires the student to draw upon a number of previously gained skills, as well as those covered in the specific module, to solve or complete the activity.

Every curriculum module uses the architecture developed by the NCE/AME project. The module architecture relies on a team process to identify critical competencies, which serve as the foundation for developing all learning activities. Assessment is embedded in every level. Before formal testing occurs, each module is subjected to two review processes: one by industry experts and one by academic experts. Once a module passes the expert reviews, two rounds of formal testing by educators and students take place. Alpha testing confirms that instructional activities are appropriate and workable in the classroom for instructors and students. The follow-up beta testing measures the impact on student learning and reports student achievement levels related to the activities (competencies). A total of 31 modules were developed and pilot-tested at 20 colleges located in 13 states. A facilitator guide and a participant journal accompany each module.

The module architecture and development methodology have been successfully used to create curricula for K-12 and associate degree courses in virtually all academic disciplines.

The capstone project required of each student for completing the degree program is focused, specific, and designed to meet an actual, rather than artificial, industry need. The capstone experience can occur in the participant's existing employment environment or in a local model manufacturing facility (a teaching factory). Typically, capstone experiences involve a team composed of other participants, experienced co-workers, or some mix of the two.

NCE/AME also organizes and delivers a series of special education and training sessions.

Familiarization institutes. One- or two-day institutes offered quarterly to familiarize high school and community college faculty and counselors with the NCE/AME modules, module architecture, and pilot-testing experiences.

Awareness workshops. A series of workshops held at Sinclair and local manufacturing companies to build awareness of and appreciation for career opportunities in manufacturing.

Technical assistance workshops. Technical assistance workshops designed to meet specific customer needs and then delivered under a fee-for-service structure to other educational institutions throughout the United States.

Summer training workshops. Sinclair-sponsored training for engineering technology, science, and mathematics faculty in which community college and university faculty work hand-in-hand with industry participants to learn about new technology in the areas of rapid prototyping, work cell simulation, and process control.

Why This Approach?

Local leaders had observed that manufacturing had changed dramatically in recent years, fueled by technological advances and streamlined business practices. As a result, they were looking for workers with new skills that could help power the Dayton-area economy. Although this idea was not new to most technician educators, educational systems had not made the necessary educational reforms calculated to produce the new skilled technician.

Students being introduced to CNC Control in preparation for a CNC programming class.

PARTNERS

Dayton Tooling and Machining Association. A 310-member organization serving the tooling and machining industry. Helped validate curriculum.

Makino. Contracted with the AIM Center to develop modules (using the module architecture and development methodology) tailored to their specific company needs.

University of Dayton. Helped with development of instructional module content and pilot-testing.

Institute of Advanced Manufacturing Science. Contracted with the AIM Center to develop a module (using the module architecture and development methodology) that they would use to train their customers.

Project Management Institute. Contracted with the AIM Center to develop continuing education courses (using the module architecture and development methodology) that they are to identify through a survey of their members.

Midwest Center for Advanced Technological Education (MCATE), Purdue University. Helped disseminate materials.

Computer Integrated Manufacturing in Higher Education Alliance (CIM/HE).

Western Michigan University. Provided a cluster captain for the Manufacturing Systems and Automation Cluster.

University of Nebraska. Provided a cluster captain for the Enterprise Integration Cluster.

Mott Community College. Hosted faculty workshops and supported curriculum development.

York Technical College. Contracted with the center to provide faculty development workshops in modular curriculum development.

The work-related problems were the best and most unique part of the module. This made the activities, which were not really new to physics instructors, seem new.
—*Instructor*

The National Center of Excellence is addressing this need by aligning the customer (manufacturing companies) with the supplier (secondary schools, community colleges, and universities) to ensure that the product (knowledgeable employees) meets the requirements of the customer. Graduates learn not only new skills, but also processes for continuous skill improvement. NCE/AME worked to define levels of partnerships necessary to address these needs. Sinclair Community College and the University of Dayton have had particularly strong ties over the years. Built on personal and professional relationships at the administrative level, the two institutions (one public and the other private, Catholic) now offer a dual admissions program. Other corporate and education partners support the curriculum process and skills-training verification.

Influences on Program Development

After specifying the target job description for the graduate, a large group of faculty and staff from Sinclair Community College and the University of Dayton developed the initial list of competencies that a graduate should demonstrate. The major resources used include:

- Society of Manufacturing Engineers (SME) Curricula 2000 and Curricula 2002 documents, which outline the recommended content of any type of college-level program in fields related to manufacturing engineering, including the associate degree in manufacturing engineering technology
- Recommended 12th grade standards of the National Science Education Standards
- Recommended 12th grade standards of the National Council of Teachers of Mathematics
- Standards and recommendations of the American Mathematical Association of Two-Year Colleges

- SCANS competencies developed by the U.S. Department of Labor Secretary's Commission on Achieving Necessary Skills
- Several voluntary industry skill standards developed under the guidance of the National Skill Standards Board, particularly those called Advanced High Performance Manufacturing, Computer-Aided Drafting and Design (CADD), and Machining
- Washington State Manufacturing Technology Standards as developed and promulgated by the Manufacturing Technology Advisory Group, Seattle, Washington, 1995
- Machining and Metalworking Skill Standards as promulgated by the National Institute for Metalworking Skills (NIMS) and the National Tooling and Machining Association (NTMA)
- *Setting the Standard: A Handbook on Skill Standards for the High Tech Industry,* Workforce Skills Project, American Electronics Association, Santa Clara, California, 1994
- National Photonics Skills Standard for Technicians, Center for Occupational Research and Development, Waco, Texas, 1995
- *Sinclair Community College Bulletin,* 1995–96, Sinclair Community College, Dayton, Ohio
- *University of Dayton Bulletin,* 1995–96, University of Dayton, Dayton, Ohio.
- Selected competencies developed by the Miami Valley Tech Prep Consortium

Emphasis was placed on solid foundations in mathematics, science, communications, teamwork, manufacturing processes, materials science, automation, manufacturing systems, controls, quality management, production and inventory control, the product realization process, and enterprise integration.

The proposed list of competencies includes a much broader set of topics than has been typical in manufacturing engineering technology programs that focus on metalworking technologies. Enterprise integration includes the funda-

Fifteen Learning Statements

The module architecture and the pedagogy incorporated in the modules are based on the following 15 learning statements. The statements present the philosophy of learning adopted by the NCE/AME project team.

1. Learning is a lifelong process.
2. Learners construct their own knowledge and understanding of the world in which they live.
3. Learners search for tools to help understand their experiences.
4. Learners come to classrooms with different backgrounds, knowledge, skills, values, and experiences.
5. Learners have preferred modes of learning. Activities need to be structured so learners can utilize their preferred mode of learning, as well as have the opportunities to develop skills in using other modes.
6. Learners must be active participants in the learning process.
7. Learners need opportunities for real, hands-on and/or concrete experiences.
8. Learners should be challenged to build on past experiences to create new schemes or structures.
9. Learners should be allowed to explore, experiment, and discover.
10. If learners see the value of the learning, they will become active seekers of knowledge and will assume responsibility for learning.
11. Learners grasp the meaning of concepts more easily when they go from whole to part rather than part to whole.
12. Learners need opportunities to develop metacognitive and interpersonal skills and need time to reflect on their learning.
13. Learning to learn is an important skill that needs to be emphasized in all content areas.
14. All areas of development, which include the areas of motor, thinking, language, and social-emotional-skills, are used when a learner is in a learning situation.
15. A higher degree of learning occurs when the experiences are integrated, which involves many different subjects and skills being used at the same time. Learning is not integrated when each subject is treated separately, and learners are expected to integrate the subject matter and skill at some future date.

Guiding Principles for Curriculum Development

Prior to beginning the actual development of instructional modules, the project team defined a set of seven guiding principles that authors are expected to adhere to as they develop each module. To the extent possible, each of the guiding principles should be evident within each module. In this way, participants gain valuable continuity of experience and reinforcement of these important principles. They become more internalized as the participant progresses through the program.

1. Scientific Methods

Program Goal: Use scientific processes to formulate questions and plan investigations; collect and interpret data; formulate and revise explanations and models using logic and evidence; analyze alternative explanations and models proposed by others; communicate and defend scientific conclusions.

2. Written Communication

Program Goal: Demonstrate the ability to write with a purpose in different formats for a variety of audiences and to organize, synthesize, and communicate the significance of their technical or non-technical information.

3. Oral Communication

Program Goal: Effectively communicate with, listen to, and respond to others interpersonally, in teams or through presentations.

4. Teamwork

Program Goal: Demonstrate a cooperative effort in a group to evaluate, solve problems, and develop and implement plans and procedures.

5. Diversity and Fair-Mindedness

Program Goal: Demonstrate a willingness to fair-mindedly assess the moral viewpoints or reasoning of others, regardless of one's own bias, as well as a willingness to put oneself imaginatively in the place of others in order to genuinely understand them.

6. Global and Societal Awareness

Program Goal: Demonstrate an awareness of the relationship between each module and the local, national, or global community.

7. Career Applications

Program Goal: Demonstrate how major concepts and processes of each module apply to careers in science and technology.

mentals of business management at a level appropriate for a manufacturing engineering technician for understanding the place of her or his work in the enterprise. In addition, competencies were included appropriate to grades 11 and 12 in mathematics, science, communication, and teamwork skills.

A secondary consideration was the articulation of the associate degree program with a bachelor's of science degree program in engineering technology.

The project's national visiting committee was also helpful in guiding activities. Members of the committee represented community college leaders, professional association administrators, private industry executives, an accreditation organization official, and government supervisors.

Student Recruitment

The National Center of Excellence's work to date has focused on curriculum development and assisting Sinclair Community College with establishing this program as a model installation. To date Sinclair has established a good record with the first students entering an associate degree program in manufacturing engineering technology in the fall of 1997 and the first graduates gaining their associate degrees in the spring of 1999. Sinclair is pioneering the use of modularized curriculum in a traditional lecture course and is committed to converting to a totally modularized program once all of the modular materials are available. Fall 2003 is the targeted date for total installation of the new novel curriculum program.

Students for this program are being recruited from a number of different sources including the existing tech prep programs in the Miami Valley Tech Prep Consortium schools. Presently, the college has the highest tech prep enrollment in the state, in part because it begins making links with students in middle school through coordinated career development programs and Tech Prep Awareness Days. Some of the Tech Prep schools use Center modules, so students will be familiar with the opportunities the college offers.

Sinclair Community College's dual enrollment agreement with the University of Dayton will grow as another enrollment source, particularly for underrepresented groups who are targeted by the television promotions, public service announcements, and videos aimed at recruiting women and minorities into engineering technology.

Unexpected Outcomes

The module assessment process was refined to include an analysis of students' cognitive growth. As a result, beta testing of the module architecture has produced results that are new, interesting, and potentially quite important. First, there is no statistically significant difference in the total scores of minorities and non-minorities for authentic learning tasks and transfer activities. Minority students represented four major ethnic groups: African American, Asian American, Hispanic American, and Native American. Second, in an independent assessment of authentic learning task total scores, females received significantly higher ratings than did males.

With separate grant funding, the college applied the module architecture approach to five other divisions at the college, resulting in ten additional modules, including the traditional general education curriculum.

The community college partnership with a university is helping parents change their notions of manufacturing to recognize that today's new manufacturing is a safer, cleaner, better work envi-

MAJOR ACHIEVEMENTS

Associate of Science in Manufacturing Technology. Developed new program with first students graduating in June 1999.

Competency-based modules. Developed 31 competency-based modules, each with complete student performance assessments embedded in the curriculum, and each including a facilitator guide and a participant journal. Altogether, the modules for the associate degree contain 175 separate competencies that were selected from a list of 800 relevant competencies identified in the initial rounds of industry wants and needs analysis. The team created a model module, with standardized wording and clear instructions to the writer, to make materials consistent across the curriculum.

Multidisciplinary applications. Created processes and methodology applicable in other fields at the college, including the general education curriculum.

Philosophical foundation for curriculum development. Developed 15 learning statements and seven guiding principles for curriculum development.

ronment than in the past. Some Ohio Tech Prep sites are using the modules to meet the needs of applied academics advocates. Interest in the module architecture exceeded expectations and staff are in demand as presenters and technical assistance providers to colleges in Virginia, South Carolina, and California. They provide similar services to industry in the Dayton area.

Recognition

The Process Control module won a Society for Technical Communication Award of Merit in February 2000. Sinclair recognized the AIM Center's contributions in developing the ATE/NCE Architecture and Curriculum Development Methodology, which affected how the entire college updates and revises curriculum in every discipline it offers.

Students using a Computerized Coordinate Measuring Machine during an Authentic Learning Task (ALT) in Quality.

[The modules] provided me with a much broader base of teamwork and activities for classroom interaction.

—Instructor

College Commitment

Sinclair's president, provost, and vice president for instruction are strongly committed to the National Center.

Leveraged Funds

The AIM Center has not taken the approach of leveraging funds within grant accounting. Rather, it takes on each assignment as a project and institutes project accounting practices. This is felt to be critical to efforts to sustain the National Center of Excellence without total dependence on grant funding. The Center also treats each grant as a project, utilizing personnel across several projects without penalizing any one project at the expense of another.

What's Next?

The National Center of Excellence expects to continue its consultations with other colleges to spread its curriculum design more thoroughly nationwide. It also plans to continue its work in applying its model throughout all departments in the college. Funds generated by the sale of the modules as well as fees from training sessions and technical assistance will be used to sustain the center's work. The center has also committed resources to develop a business venture in selling services based on the application of the module architecture and development methodology to commercial training materials. Through NSF grant funding, the center will complete the remaining 39 modules required for the new, novel associate degree program in manufacturing engineering technology.

Materials Produced by the Project

Carroll, John, Fred Thomas, Arthur Ross, and Marta Gruesbeck. 1998. *Forces and their effects: facilitator guide.* Dayton, Ohio: Sinclair Community College National Center of Excellence for Advanced Manufacturing.

Carroll, John, Fred Thomas, Arthur Ross, and Marta Gruesbeck. 1998. *Forces and their effects: participant journal.* Dayton, Ohio: Sinclair Community College National Center of Excellence for Advanced Manufacturing.

Constable, Gordon, Mary Kay Hershey, James Houdeshelle, and Lynn Seery. *Quality foundations: facilitator guide.* Dayton, Ohio: Sinclair Community College National Center of Excellence for Advanced Manufacturing.

Houdeshelle, James, and Fred Thomas. 1996. Integration of liberal studies into the manufacturing curriculum: The use of guiding principles in curriculum development. In *Preparing world class manufacturing professionals,* SME Proceedings of the International Conference on Education in Manufacturing. Dearborn, Mich: Society of Manufacturing Engineers.

Mize, Cinda, and Donna Krile. 1997 (January). *Alpha pilot test of curriculum modules.* Dayton, Ohio: Sinclair Community College National Center of Excellence for Advanced Manufacturing Education.

Mize, Cinda, and Donna Krile. 1997 (March). *Alpha pilot test of curriculum modules.* Dayton, Ohio: Sinclair Community College National Center of Excellence for Advanced Manufacturing Education.

Mott, Robert L. 1996 (April). Issues Related to TAC of ABET Accreditation for the Proposed Associate Degree Program in Manufacturing Engineering Technology. Dayton, Ohio: Sinclair Community College. Duplicated.

Mott, Robert L. 1996 (April). National Center of Excellence for Advanced Manufacturing Education Curriculum Development Process. Dayton, Ohio: Sinclair Community College. Duplicated.

National Center of Excellence for Advanced Manufacturing Education. 1995 (November). A Structured Approached to Competency-Based Curriculum Development. Executive Summary. Dayton, Ohio: Sinclair Community College.

National Center of Excellence for Advanced Manufacturing Education. 1996. Curriculum Design for a Novel Associate Degree Program in Manufacturing Engineering Technology. Dayton, Ohio: Sinclair Community College. Duplicated.

National Center of Excellence for Advanced Manufacturing Education. 1996 (July). Curriculum Outline. Dayton, Ohio: Sinclair Community College. Duplicated.

National Center of Excellence for Advanced Manufacturing Education. [1996]. Relationships Between National Skill Standards and NCE/AME Curriculum. Dayton, Ohio: Sinclair Community College. Duplicated.

NCE/AME Project Team. 1997 (April). Architectural Patterns in Curriculum Development. White Paper. Dayton, Ohio: Sinclair Community College AIM Center. Duplicated.

Associate of Science in Manufacturing Technology Competency-based Modules

Title	Author(s)
1. Basic DC Circuits	Harmit Kaur
2. Basic Material Removal	Barbara Andregg, John Clarke, W. Alan Lynam, Nick Martin, Thomas Salvaggio
3. Basic Statistical Variation	Barbara Carruth, Bob Chaney, Jan Kledzik, Cathy Mulligan
4. Computer Numerical Control	Tom Boersma, Tarun Gupta
5. Conceptual Design	Phil Doepker, Brian Knouff, Patrick MacLellan
6. Consistent Work Methods and Build to Demand	Julie Hatton, William Valentine
7. Customer Satisfaction	Linda Alexander, Pat Galitz, James Houdeshell
8. Describing Position, Velocity, and Acceleration	Bob Chaney, Marta Gruesbeck, Fred Thomas
9. Electrical and Electronic Controls	Tarun Gupta, John Mason
10. Forces and Their Effects	John Carroll, Marta Gruesbeck, Arthur Ross, Fred Thomas
11. Geometric Dimensioning and Tolerancing	Kay Cornelius, Barry Grady, James Houdeshell, Fred Thomas, Don Wendeln
12. Introduction to Just-In-Time (JIT)	Ronald Caldwell, David Harrison, Saul Young, Reginald Yu-Lee
13. Introduction to World-Class Manufacturing	Shepherd Anderson, Robert Mott
14. Kanban and Pull Systems	Julie Hatton, Chet Logue, William Valentine
15. Metal Forming and Joining	Perry Carter, Raymond Dekeyser, W. Alan Lynam, Thomas Salvaggio
16. Metallic Materials	Cynthia Barnicki, James Houdeshell
17. Non-Metallic Materials	William Maston, Joseph Neville, Margaret Pinnell
18. Performance Measures	Raymond Carpenter, Thomas Lagerstrom, Ken Merkel, Larry Shaw, Terry Stentz
19. Plastics Manufacturing Processes and Materials	Per Flem, William Maston, Joseph Neville, Robert Willison
20. Precision, Accuracy, and Tolerance	Kay Cornelius, Art Goss, Marta Gruesbeck, Tom Peterson
21. Principles of Manufacturing Processes	Shepherd Anderson, Jack Steeves
22. Principles of Production and Inventory Control	Mark Gooch, Julie Hatton, William Valentine
23. Process Flow and Lead Time Reduction	Julie Hatton, William Valentine
24. Process Control	Gordon Constable, James Houdeshell, Tom Peterson, Lynn Seery
25. Professional Development	Shepherd Anderson
26. Quality Foundations	Gordon Constable, Mary Kay Hershey, James Houdeshell, Lynn Seery
27. Robots and Programmable Logic Controllers	Tarun Gupta
28. Statistical Distributions	Barbara Carruth, Bob Chaney, Tom Peterson
29. Teamwork	David Bodary, James Houdeshell, Ned Young
30. Tooling for Manufacturing	Jon Beeman, Donald Book, George Comber, Kent Kohkonen
31. Units and Conversions	Kay Cornelius, Steve Crain, Cathy Mulligan, Tom Whitehead

Pilot-Testing of NCE/AME Modules

Colleges

Alfred State College-SUNY		Alfred	NY
Arkansas Technical University		Russellville	AR
Central Ohio Technical College		Newark	OH
Central Piedmont Community College		Charlotte	NC
Cuyahoga Community College		Cleveland	OH
DeKalb Technical Institute		Covington	GA
Delaware Technical Community College		Dover	DE
Delaware Technical Community College		Newark	DE
Delaware Technical Community College		Wilmington	DE
Essex County College		Newark	NJ
Iowa Western Community College		Council Bluffs	IA
Miami University		Oxford	OH
New England Institute of Technology		Warwick	RI
North Carolina A & T State University		Greensboro	NC
Northern Illinois University		De Kalb	IL
Northern Kentucky University		Highland Heights	KY
Northwestern Michigan College		Traverse City	MI
Oklahoma State University-Okmulgee		Okmulgee	OK
Patrick Henry Community College		Martinsville	VA
Portland Community College		Portland	OR
Purdue University-Technology		W. Lafayette	IN
St. Louis Community College		Florissant Valley	MO
Sinclair Community College		Dayton	OH
Southeast Community College		Lincoln	NE
South Seattle Community College		Seattle	WA
Toledo Technical Academy		Toledo	OH
University of Central Florida		Orlando	FL
University of Dayton		Dayton	OH
Wayne State University		Detroit	MI
Westark Community College		Fort Smith	AR
Western Michigan University		Grand Rapids	MI

High Schools

Catholic Central High School		Springfield	OH
Centerville High School	(Dayton)	Centerville	OH
Detroit School of Industrial Arts		Detroit	MI
Fairmont High School	(Dayton)	Kettering	OH
Fenwick Catholic High School		Middletown	OH
Kettering High School	(Dayton)	Kettering	OH
Manufacturing Technology Academy		Traverse City	MI
Miamisburg High School	(Dayton)	Miamisburg	OH
Northridge High School	(Dayton)	Dayton	OH

Hawkeye Community College
Waterloo, Iowa

Validation and Implementation of a Coordinated Precision Agricultural Curriculum

▶ **FOCUS**
▶ Certificate and associate degrees in precision agriculture
▶ Emphasis on math, science, and applications of emerging technologies

College Environment

Hawkeye Community College is located in the southern city limits of Waterloo, Iowa, part of the Cedar Valley Area. The area is known for a strong work ethic, affordable housing, a commitment to education, and a wide variety of community activities. Serving a wide agricultural area, the college offers a comprehensive set of programs and services: arts and sciences (transfer) program, including a variety of options and concentrations; 43 vocational-technical programs; adult and continuing education, community programs and services; customized training and retraining for business and industry as economic development initiatives; and numerous general interest classes. Economic development and advancing technology dictate changes in curriculum emphases that result in a variety of partnerships with business, industry, agriculture, and other elements of the public and private sectors.

Since the inception of its transfer program in 1992, the college (formerly called Hawkeye Institute of Technology) has had a 97 percent credit enrollment growth. Enrollment in 1998 was 3,944, with 53 percent of the students enrolled in the arts and sciences program. Approximately 47 percent of the students are full time, taking 12 or

Hawkeye Community College
1501 East Orange Road
PO Box 8015
Waterloo, IA 50704-8015
Ph: 319/296-2320
www.hawkeye.cc.ia.us
Acting President: Charles Ullom

Contacts
Terry Brase, Project Director
Kirkwood Community College
Agricultural Sciences
6301 Kirkwood Blvd. SW
Cedar Rapids, IA 52406
Ph: 319/398-5458
Fax: 319/398-5611
E-mail: tbrase@kirkwood.cc.ia.us

Charlie Gregory, Assistant Project Director
Hawkeye Community College
Agriculture and Power Technologies
1501 East Orange Road
Waterloo, IA 50704-8015
Ph: 319/296-4008
Fax: 319/296-1028
E-mail: cgregory@hawkeye.cc.ia.us

Bob Welch, Assistant Project Director
Lansing Community College
422 N. Washington Square, Dept. 3600
Lansing, MI 48933
Ph: 517/483-9675
Fax: 517/483-9619.
E-mail: rwelch@lansing.cc.mi.us

Program Web Address
www.ag.hawkeye.cc.ia.us

more credits each semester. Fifty-five percent are female. Eighty-nine percent of the students are white, non-Hispanic, and 9 percent are African American, non-Hispanic. Native Iowans make up 99 percent of the student body.

The college's open campus offers more than 3,300 day and evening continuing education programs, as well as customized, on-site training for business and industry. More than 6,000 new jobs have been created since 1984 through training agreements under Iowa's industry new jobs training program. The college manages a 220-acre farm laboratory.

The college operates two off-campus centers. The Evansdale Center offers a manufacturing technology program dedicated to training, retraining, and providing skill enhancement opportunities for individuals employed in manufacturing companies. The Martin Luther King, Jr. Center includes full college services, including degree-related courses, Iowa Public Television courses, distance learning courses, basic computer workshops, adult basic education, general educational development, high school credit classes, professional and personal development, student services, and computerized library services.

The college maintains a lively interaction with a wide scope of community organizations. Its 10-county, 2,742-square-mile service area has an estimated population of 200,000, with 63 percent residing in Black Hawk County. Major employers

Students get practical hands-on experience in using GPS in agriculture applications. Shown here are students taking soil samples in a Hawkeye CC Farm Laboratory field while other students use a GPS mounted on a 4-wheel drive vehicle to record the latitude/longitude position.

include John Deere and Company, Midwest Power Systems, IBP, U.S. West Communications, and Nestle Beverage USA.

Program Profile

Upon a previous effort funded by the National Science Foundation that produced a two-year associate of applied science degree in agriculture and food technology, Hawkeye Community College built a new agriculture program. This new effort partners Hawkeye Community College with seven other community colleges to validate and implement a coordinated curriculum in precision agriculture. Precision agriculture is defined as the utilization of all aspects of emerging technologies—such as biotechnology, computers and telecommunications, animal technology, and precision farming—that allow an agriculturist to organize and maintain data for making decisions about precise production units. The seven colleges participating with Hawkeye are Kirkwood Community College in Iowa; Lansing Community College in Michigan; Carl Sandburg College and Parkland College in Illinois; Ridgewater College in Minnesota; Southwest Wisconsin Technical College in Wisconsin; and Vincennes University in Indiana.

The curriculum incorporates modules and courses in precision farming, environmental science, biotechnology, and technology, along with a core of mathematics and science courses. The seven colleges purchased equipment, reviewed the curriculum materials, received training, and then implemented the curriculum on their own campuses. They also provided professional development activities for teachers in kindergarten through high school. The seven colleges are responsible for developing certificate and degree programs or integrating the new curriculum into their current programs. Each of the colleges has established a formal link to at least one K-12 school and one university. Collaborative connections with the K-12 sector are designed to strengthen math and science instruction. With the universities, staff efforts center on creating articulation agreements and enhancing pre-service and in-service training for teachers with technical updates on precision agriculture.

Two of the seven college partners have special roles because of their individual strengths. Kirkwood Community College, through its Advanced Technology Environmental Education Center, provides leadership and assistance in developing environmental education courses integrated into agricultural programs at the participating colleges. Kirkwood staff review all new curricula to ensure that environmental health and safety technologies are addressed appropriately. A new agriculture technology building at Kirkwood supports the advancement of precision agriculture education. Lansing Community College, because of its focus on career-based education, provides leadership and assistance in developing Geographic Information Systems (GIS) integration into at collaborating colleges. It also designed and implemented a one-year precision farming program.

A network called the Precision Agriculture Education Network (PrAEN) aids in the development process across the colleges. Network users include partners in K-12 schools, community colleges, and universities as well as industry representatives. Other communication approaches used by the staff include biannual conferences and a project Web site.

Out of this effort will come a coordinated precision agriculture curriculum that provides a seamless career pathway for K-16 students that stresses math and science skills necessary for technologically advanced careers.

Why This Approach?

In the last four years, the technology side of agriculture and the food industry has evolved rapidly. In their pursuit to protect natural resources in agriculture, environmentalists are discovering the value of Global Positioning Systems (GPS) and GIS and other technology. The availability of low-cost computing power, the GPS, and improved understanding of crop growth allow site specific crop management. These developments make it increasingly possible for farmers to manage crops and lands more precisely.

Even so, production, service, processing, and retail workers have limited access to the knowledge held by researchers, engineers, and product developers. Most community college or undergraduate curricula today inadequately present the full scope of learning and application required by the industry. According to business and industry, the current

PARTNERS

Kirkwood Community College. Leadership and assistance in developing environmental education courses and ensuring that environmental health and safety technologies are addressed appropriately.

Lansing Community College. Leadership and assistance in GIS integration.

Carl Sandburg College. Curriculum validation and implementation.

Parkland College. Curriculum validation and implementation.

Ridgewater College. Curriculum validation and implementation.

Southwest Wisconsin Technical College. Curriculum validation and implementation.

Vincennes University. Curriculum validation and implementation.

ArcView. GIS software donations, faculty training, and guidance in curriculum development.

Indiana State University. Faculty training in GIS.

Farmer's Software, Inc. Precision agriculture workshop presentations and curriculum development assistance.

Local cooperatives. Opportunities for students to witness the tools of precision agriculture in operation.

workforce has either a strong computer background or a strong agricultural background but not a blend of both fields. By developing a systematic precision agriculture curriculum, a college can offer an integrated background in agriculture and technology.

Precision agriculture makes use of current and emerging technologies to produce better or more desirable crops and livestock in a more efficient and cost-controlled manner. For example, GPS/GIS can be used to map the yield rates and soil conditions of a plot of land and then to apply variable levels of the appropriate soil conditioners and fertilizers. Bioengineering can be used to modify plant and animal characteristics to create more disease-resistant strains.

As society faces these complex technology-based challenges, there is a need for educators to cooperate and form partnerships across all levels of education as well as with agriculture industries. These partners need to promote and support the development of awareness, knowledge, understanding, and application of technology for students, the current workforce, and educators at all levels in mathematics, science, and agriculture.

Influences on Program Development
The project is a network of collaborating institutions, all of which have contributed their expertise and experience to its development. The community colleges and the linked institutions and schools with which the colleges work include those listed below:

- Hawkeye Community College: Iowa State University; University of Northern Iowa; East High School, Waterloo; Orange Elementary, Waterloo; Dike Community School; Union Community School, LaPorte City and Dysart; and Vinton Community School
- Kirkwood Community College: Iowa State University and College Community High School, Cedar Rapids
- Lansing Community College: Eastern Michigan State University and Livingston Community School
- Carl Sandburg College: Western Illinois University and ROWVA High School, Oneida
- Parkland College: University of Illinois and FCAE District 7
- Ridgewater College: University of Minnesota, St. Paul, and Willmar Community Schools
- Southwest Wisconsin Technical College: University of Wisconsin, Platteville, and Lancaster Community School
- Vincennes University: Purdue University and North Knox Community School, Bicknell, Indiana

Other organizations have influenced the project's development. The PrAEN network collaborated with the National Association of Agricultural Educators to develop and implement professional development workshops in precision farming. Use of the PrAEN curriculum broadened when the Hawkeye project director participated in a mentoring project with Phi Theta Kappa, the two-year college honor society. The Phosphorus and Potassium Institute provided expertise and materials to the participating schools, and the Advanced Technological Environmental Education Center provided environmental information and a curriculum specialist.

Two companies were extremely helpful. Deere and Company and Rockwell International provided equipment and technical expertise in building the initial list of competencies and skills that formed the base for the PrAEN curriculum.

Student Recruitment
Recruiting activities were extremely important for this project. Agriculture has a shortage of educated technicians because the industry has been perceived as low tech and high labor. With the emerging technologies in agriculture, this perception is starting to change, but it takes a dedicated recruitment and outreach effort to spread the word. College recruitment activities have had the dual goal of informing people about the agriculture and food technology program and educating people about the emerging technologies in agriculture and the impor-

Students collect a boundary with the Rockwell Vision System.

tance of science and math in the curriculum. Specific college efforts include:

- conducting community education activities such as GPS Yield Monitor Field Demonstrations. These have been successful in getting the general public on college grounds or on the institution's farm to witness the connection between the discipline and technology
- presenting at statewide conferences such as the Iowa Soybean Association Ag Tech Conference. This has been helpful in displaying the college's expertise with technology in agriculture
- visiting high schools, a mainstay of the recruitment process that provides opportunities to work with teachers to create practical demonstrations for students. These visits allow college staff to show students technology applications in agriculture, identify careers in the field, and name sources of appropriate education. The staff do not hard-sell the college's program during these meetings, but the visits have proven to be effective recruiting tools
- hosting or co-hosting informal training sessions for agriculture instructors at the Future Farmers of America Agricultural Science Fairs. These sessions have been effective because of the influence these instructors have in advising students

Unexpected Outcomes

Enrollment has increased in all agriculture programs at the college. At the project's outset, staff were concerned that the new program would pull students out of other agriculture curricula. In fact, not only is agriculture and food technology the fastest-growing program on campus, but also many students have indicated that they are enrolling in the college's other agriculture programs because of the technology available to them. These developments have stimulated interest from other college departments. Staff from other departments have requested assistance from the project leaders to help show how emerging technologies can be applied in their instructional disciplines.

Nationwide, interest is growing in the use of the PrAEN curriculum. In answer to many requests,

MAJOR ACHIEVEMENTS

Agriculture and food technology two-year associate degree program. The new program was approved by the Hawkeye Community College Board of Trustees (April 1996) and by the Iowa Department of Education (August 1996), and the college offered the curriculum for the first time in fall 1996. The program of study is available on the project Web site, which also contains a listing of courses, course descriptions, a suggested schedule of courses, and current course guides/syllabi for some classes.

Precision agriculture curriculum. This new curriculum serves as a model for participating colleges. Using the curriculum created in the first project phase, college curriculum specialists created a set of adaptable modules that can be used as stand-alone courses or as parts of an existing course. These modules are introduction to GPS/GIS, data collection, data analysis, data generation, and other emerging technologies. Each of these modules contains sub-modules that cover a specific topic, with lesson plans, lecture outlines, supplementary laboratory exercises, and a list of multimedia material. This information is available in different forms: printed booklet, CD-ROM, and on the Internet.

Network of community colleges, K-12 schools, universities, and industries. To validate the curriculum and implement it broadly, staff shaped an active network of seven community colleges from the Upper Midwest. The role of the network colleges is to:

- update equipment related to emerging technologies of precision farming based on the recommendations of Hawkeye Community College
- participate in training on the updated equipment and precision farming concepts
- apply and evaluate project curriculum materials to determine their effectiveness and provide assistance in editing and improving them
- take on a set of instructional units for further development

continued on next page...

...continued

- share equipment and resources with collaborating K-12 schools to enhance student math, science, and technology preparedness
- collaborate with one or more universities to improve coursework and to establish possible articulation procedures
- interact with industry partners to establish competencies required of employable graduates

Professional development activities for K-12 teachers. To enhance the science and technology skills of K-12 teachers and their ability to teach effectively precision agriculture, Hawkeye Community College held a series of three- or four-day professional development workshops where teachers received hands-on experiences using precision agriculture equipment. They were given practice in activities that they can use with their students. Many participant teachers have created instructional units through the workshops. The Hawkeye Community College is collecting these units to share with the project's collaborating colleges.

I grew up on a farm and always thought that I would work on a farm, especially after getting an associate degree in ag business management in 1978. [After being laid off from a farm cooperative during the farm crisis of the early 1980s], I began to read about the need for ag personnel again but also had heard about the use of computers and satellites. I knew I had a lot of catching up to do. The courses I took gave me experience and industry contacts to get a job.
—Student in precision agriculture program, now employed as a GLPS manager for an agricultural cooperative

the college will distribute the curriculum after final revisions and validation. Information on program development is provided at the PrAEN Web site.

Recognition
The precision agriculture project has received national notice through presentations at international, national, and regional conferences and visits to four other two-year colleges in the United States and Canada. A number of published papers highlighted the project. Contacts with geographically diverse universities and two-year colleges continue. The project's director was named the Outstanding Iowa Community College Faculty Member of 1997, based in part on his work in precision agriculture.

College Commitment
Evidence of the college's commitment to the program is clear in its willingness to share costs and its approval of the curriculum as part of its standing offerings to students. The college has endorsed the

agriculture department's new vision: "Educating agriculturists for an ever-changing world." In support of this endorsement, the college has underwritten improvements to the School Farm Laboratory, including new equipment (such as tractors, feeding equipment, and wagons), and it has provided additional land to ensure that students get extensive hands-on experience. In addition, a new swine facility with the latest technology is being planned as well as a multi-purpose structure that will be used for a variety of purposes related in part to the interests of the agriculture department.

Leveraged Funds
In addition to the participating schools who have provided matching equipment funds, a variety of outside groups provided generous donations of funds, equipment, software, and other items. John Deere and Company donated $250,000 for the creation of a technologically advanced computer laboratory called the John Deere Advanced Technical Center. (The college matched these donations with $350,000.) Farmer's Software, Inc. provided a collection of equipment and software valued at more than $10,000 to support the precision agriculture program, including Megellan DGPS Coast Guard Beacon Receiver, LabelWorks UBI Quickscan Scanner, MapInfo, FarmGPS, FarmLAB, FarmHMS

(Harvest Mapping Software), SGIS Mapping Suite, and Pen-based Toshiba. Environmental Research Systems, Inc. provided additional software worth $125,000, including ArcView 3.0, Spatial Analyst, Network Analyst, and 3-D Analyst. Rockwell International donated more than $200,000 worth of GPS equipment, GIS software, and technical support to participating schools in the project.

Lessons Learned

Agriculture is an industry with thousands of years of tradition. Every 50 to 100 years technical advancements seem to surface that allow major changes to take place. Although there are many individuals who are resistant to change, the change is inevitable and for the most part provides safer, more economical, and more abundant food.

The technological advances now taking place in agriculture require a higher degree of science and math skills than ever before. The agriculture industry faces limitations in its ability to make use of this technology, not because of cost or availability, but because it lacks an educated workforce that can make use of the technology. Education is the key. Teachers and instructors must be trained not only in the use of GPS, but also in the math, science, analytical, computer, and GIS skills to use it for decision making. They must teach their students to do the same.

The learning curve of these new technological skills is high. The learning curve for using those skills for appropriate decision making is even higher. The project at Hawkeye and its college partners suggests that a guided approach in developing programs and use of curriculum material is needed. Schools wanting to implement more than a overview of geospatial technologies will require mentors, professional development workshops, and assistance by industry.

What's Next?

The curriculum is a standing part of the full college offerings. In the future, the staff anticipate conducting the following additional activities:

- integrate technology in other technical programs at the college
- distribute curriculum materials nationally
- develop a trainers program to assist interested colleges in applying the curriculum and its principles in their college programs,

similar to the ATE-supported mentoring program managed by Phi Theta Kappa of which Hawkeye Community College's principal investigator is a part

Materials Produced by the Program

Among the materials produced by the program to date:

Agriculture and food technology curriculum. For other colleges interested in developing a precision agriculture program, the program of study and course descriptions for this associate degree are available at www.ag.hawkeye.cc.ia.us/Curricul.htm.

Precision agriculture curriculum. The curriculum is the primary product of this ATE grant, comprised of five modules: Introduction to GPS/GIS, Data Collection, Data Analysis, Data/Product Generation, and Other Emerging Technologies. Each module includes lesson plans, lecture outlines, lab exercises, and multimedia presentations. The lesson plans include goals, objectives, references, exploratory activities, explanatory activities, and application activities. Published in late 1999, the curriculum can be purchased by other schools.

Unit guides. These represent the basic structure of goals, objectives, activities, and references from which Applications of GPS, Applications of GIS, Ag Research, and other courses were developed. It is available at www.ag.hawkeye.cc.ia.us/Curricul.htm.

Course guides and syllabi. Guides and syllabi for various courses as developed at Hawkeye will be available at www.ag.hawkeye.cc.ia.us/Curricul.htm. Future plans are to provide hypertext links to the PrAEN curriculum for units and activities.

Additional guides. Guides for integrating precision agriculture into various courses were developed for participating schools. They include topics, lecture outlines, and lab exercises recommended for inclusion as two-to-five-day units in five different courses.

Published Papers

Development of a precision agriculture education curriculum. 1997. Proceedings of the Annual International Society of Agriculture Engineers, 12 August, Minneapolis.

Educating tomorrow's high tech farmers. 1997. *GPS World, Precision Farming Special Issue* (August).

Precision ag 101. 1997. *Farm Chemicals* 160, no. 12 (November).

GPS/GIS in agriculture. 1999. *ASEE PRISM* (American Society for Engineering Education) (February).

White paper on agricultural community concerns in precision agriculture. 1998. MidAmerica GIS Symposium, 5-7 May, Lincoln, Neb. www.ag.hawkeye.cc.ia.us/white_paper.html

Addendum to white paper, "Concerns of precision agriculture education." 1998. MidAmerica GIS Symposium, 5-7 May, Lincoln, Neb. www.ag.hawkeye.cc.ia.us/prec_ag_education.html

Note: The College acknowledges the significant contributions of its former ATE director, David Harrison.

Delta College
University Center, Michigan

Chemical Engineering Technology:
Advanced Process Operations Program

▶ **FOCUS**
- ▶ Community college/university/business collaboration
- ▶ New associate degree curriculum: Advanced Process Operation
- ▶ One year at community college, one at university

College Environment

Delta College, a public community college that opened in 1961, serves three counties in the east central portion of Michigan with a population of nearly 400,000. Nearly two-thirds are in urban areas, with 44 percent residing within the city limits of Bay City, Saginaw, and Midland. Approximately 22 percent of the residents are minority, primarily African American and Hispanic. The labor market is manufacturing-based, with the Dow Chemical Company and the Dow Corning Corporation having large plants and international corporate headquarters in Midland. Bay City's employment centers around the General Motors Corporation (GMC) and its suppliers. In Saginaw, GMC has several plants and the largest foundry concentration in the United States.

Delta College is a single campus institution, with major centers located in the cities of Bay City, Midland, and Saginaw to provide residents with convenient access to postsecondary education. The college offers 102 associate degrees and 26 certificate options. Twenty-nine percent of the students select transfer programs, and 41 percent enroll in technology programs. Sixty-nine percent of the students enroll part time; 58 percent are female; and 13 percent are minority. Over 75 percent of the

Delta College
1961 Delta Drive
University Center, MI 48710
Ph: 517/686-9000
www.delta.edu
President: Peter D. Boyse

Contacts
Edward Fisher, Principal Investigator
Chemical Engineering Department
Michigan Technological University
Ph: 906/487-3204
Fax: 906/487-3213
E-mail: edfisher@mtu.edu

Tim Collins, Co-principal Investigator
School of Technology
Michigan Technological University
Ph: 906/487-2259
Fax: 906/487-2583
E-mail: thcollin@mtu.edu

Carolyn Sandford, Co-principal Investigator
Science Division
Delta College
Ph: 517/686-9259
Fax: 517/686-8736
E-mail: clsandfo@alpha.delta.edu

Program Web Addresses
Delta College: www.delta.edu/~chm/chemical.htm
Michigan Technological University:
www.tech.mtu.edu/apo/index.html

college's graduates remain in the service district after graduation. In fall 1998, approximately 10,500 students enrolled in academic programs (6,800 FTE), with the average student taking eight credit hours.

In addition to the academic programs, Delta College's Corporate Services training division annually provides training and retraining to more than 25,000 business/industry employees throughout the state, country, and world.

Program Profile

Delta College and Michigan Technological University developed an innovative two-year degree program in chemical engineering technology: Advanced Process Operation. Drawing upon a strong partnership with Dow Corning Corporation and Dow Chemical Company, the model is appropriate for use by other colleges in other parts of the nation.

The degree program consists of a first-year program taught at Delta College, where high school articulation agreements and diversity outreach initiatives are well established. Technical chemistry, mathematics, and communication courses dominate the first-year program. In addition, students are introduced to the chemical process industries and to the fundamentals of process operations. A trip to Michigan Tech to visit the pilot plant facilities and discuss the second-year program is also usually included in the first year. Due to the proximity to manufacturing industry, students can take advantage of intern-

Fast Start students preparing for start-up of a pilot plant scale solvent recovery system in Michigan Tech's Process Simulation and Control Center (PSCC).

ships and job-shadowing in process operations. After successfully completing their first-year experience (based upon academic achievement and work-related recommendations), students take the second-year academic program at Michigan Technological University. Michigan Tech's program stresses engineering technology with a strong laboratory component leading to a capstone experience in the multipurpose pilot plant facilities of the university's Process Simulation and Control Center. Program staff organize cooperative and apprenticeship opportunities for second-year students.

The curriculum development teams included mathematics, chemistry, and physics faculty from both the college and the university, as well as representatives from local industry. Their work was informed by the voluntary skills standards prepared by the American Chemical Society as well as standards generated by the National Science Foundation. Team members also job-shadowed industry workers and managers who hire chemical processing operators to determine the skills and attitudes employers are seeking in new employees. The development effort work included identification of assessment tools and of existing training programs for process operators.

Partners Dow Corning and Dow Chemical helped develop and assess the curriculum and assisted with student recruitment and career expositions. They also provided internship sites and worked with the college to provide training facilities for students.

The model program is designed to prepare highly trained process operators who are comfortable with new process technologies and the regulations that shape these industries. Central to the program are the safety and teamwork skills that are demanded in the changing high-performance workplace of the future.

The first-year program emphasizes hands-on learning through the use of commercial kits. Faculty, for example, use Capacitor-Aided System for Teaching/ Learning Electricity (CASTLE) and Basic Electricity kits. Students construct and manipulate electric motors to help understand and work with electricity and magnetism concepts. To clarify energy conversion concepts, faculty increased the number of

Our classes have shown us how to adapt to change. Sometimes unexpected events occur in our labs, but instead of panicking, we reevaluate the entire system, brainstorm, and adapt.

—Student

genecons—hand-operated generators—used in the classrooms. Students also are exposed to Electrical Equivalent of Heat setups.

Why This Approach?

Chemical industries are struggling to find qualified new operators conversant with new federal regulations and new technologies. In response, Delta College and Michigan Technological University created a model educational program that meets or exceeds both the advanced process operator competencies required by local employers and the American Chemical Society's voluntary skill standards for process technical operators (PTO).

Influences on Program Development

The college tapped a number of resources to develop and implement the program. The American Chemical Society voluntary skill standards for process technical operators helped to determine the skills and competencies most critical for industry needs and to guide the development of the entire program. *The Process Technology Handbook and Instructor's Guide,* by Charles E. Thomas, was used as a resource for the Technical Chemistry I and II and for Introduction to Process Industries and Process Operations courses. Additional guidance came from the TTS CD-ROM series for process operator training, which contains hands-on training for students through simulations.

Important assistance came from the Partnership for the Advancement of Chemical Technologists (PACT), whose workshops helped prepare and test hands-on lab experiences that reflect industrial applications and educated chemistry faculty about how to make classroom materials compatible with work site demands. The American Association of Physics Teachers organized a series of workshops on applied physics that

PARTNERS

Delta College, science and mathematics faculty team. Developed the first-year curriculum and incorporated the ACS voluntary skill standards for process technology operators into all phases of curriculum development.

Michigan Technological University, chemical engineering faculty team. Developed the second-year curriculum, provided program and facilities for the Delta student and faculty visits to the campus, hired two new faculty to teach the second-year curriculum, and offered direct and indirect assistance to students (accessing scholarship funds, setting up study programs, and adjusting to university campus life) and to the program to ensure its success.

Dow Corning Corporation and Dow Chemical Company. Provided chemical process operator training department directors and staff to work with the college and the university and to develop and endorse the certificate and degree programs.

were attended by the college's physics faculty team members instrumental in changing the existing applied physics course. Workshops by the American Chemical Society facilitated connections with other colleges, such as Brazosport College, working in the same field in Texas.

Student Recruitment

Recruitment is an important and sometimes challenging issue for colleges offering a new program. The personal touch is often particularly important to let prospective students know about it. Delta College conducted special events for students, including a spring barbecue and school career fairs. Seeking diversity in prospective student groups, program staff invited new students who indicated an interest in a chemistry-based career as well as those who were undecided science majors. The invitations extended to the students' families as well. Industry and university representatives participated in these events. At industry partners' facilities, the college also presented career information sessions for employees and their families.

MAJOR ACHIEVEMENTS

New and re-tooled courses and certificate program. A two-semester chemistry course provides chemistry education in inorganic, organic, and polymer chemistry using hands-on/lab experiences drawn from industrial applications. An applied physics course meets new, higher technical workplace needs. A certificate program in chemical process operations was created and implemented.

New collaboration and contacts. The project enhanced collaboration among the community college, university, and industrial partners and resulted in new industrial contacts for the program and its graduates. In seeking to implement the program elsewhere, project staff also developed new academic contacts with other community colleges and universities.

New student opportunities. The college arranged internship opportunities for all students and structured a Fast Start program for minority students. Recruitment events informed others about this career and its opportunities.

High school collaboration. The project began integrating the chemical process operator into the college's Tech Prep system.

Job placement. The first graduates of the new program in advanced process operations readily found employment.

The college provided the forum for all recruitment events and worked with new students throughout the year inside and outside the classroom. Nearly every administrative department of the college provided student support services, including the Admissions Office and the Office of Academic Advising.

Not ignoring traditional recruitment venues, the college published articles describing the program and the local employer needs for trained workers in this field in area newspapers. To reach high school students, college staff held meetings with area high school principals (members of the college's Tech Prep Consortium) and area high

The chemical engineering technology program enables industry to hire new workers who understand basic processing and are equipped to deal with changes in technology.

—Student

school chemistry teachers. High school counselors were invited to the college's campus and oriented to the career potentials of the new program.

Unexpected Outcomes

Historically, the college has had excellent rapport with local business and industry, but this project intensified those relationships. Industrial partners such as Dow Chemical Company, Michigan Division, willingly provided training and equipment resources that enabled the college to offer both years of the program. Dow Corning Corporation expressed interest in establishing a consortium of community colleges in states where the company has operations in order to offer the new program and to encourage minority student participation by funding a special Fast Start program at Michigan Technological University. The company is interested in awarding scholarships to Fast Start students to stimulate program completion.

In addition, Delta College's relationship with university colleagues improved greatly. Strong university interest and effort helped second-year students complete their program on the university's campus. The college also received welfare-to-work funds from the state's Workforce Development Board for process operations and also got approval for state-funded scholarships for students entering the curriculum.

Recognition

National organizations have sought Delta College program staff as speakers at numerous meetings, including the 1995, 1996, 1997, 1998, and 1999 national ATE conferences co-sponsored by the National Science Foundation and American Association of Community Colleges in Washington, D.C. At the League for Innovation Workforce 2000 Conference, they spoke about the "hazards of multi-dimensional partnerships."

Chemical professional societies were likely sites for information sharing about the Delta College Michigan Technological University endeavor. After presenting at the 14th Biennial Conference on Chemistry Education in 1996, ATE program staff spoke again at the organization's next conference in Waterloo, Ontario. There they focused on two topics: "Active Learning in a Technical Chemistry Curriculum—General and Inorganic Chemistry and Organic Chemistry" and "Industry/Education Interface: Educating a Workforce Takes Everyone."

A presentation at the 29th Central Regional Meeting of the American Chemical Society in 1997 highlighted the program's partnership approach: "Industrial New Technical Chemistry Courses for Educational Partnership in Advanced Process Operations."

The college also hosted a field briefing for the ATE program in 1998. Attendees included the local congressman, representatives of local industry, members of the State of Michigan Educational and Technology Councils, a NSF leader, and college and university representatives. Staff have had numerous contacts with community colleges and business and industry in the state and region. All of these opportunities arose from the program's visibility, its role in meeting a very real industry need, and interest in its model of collaboration between a community college and a university.

College Commitment

The college maintained a strong commitment to the program over the three years of its ATE grant, providing at least $25,000 annually to support the program. College matching funds supported salaries and fringe benefits for some staff, faculty replacement costs for program development, support staff, recruitment staff, equipment, and supplies and materials. Since the end of the grant, and in addition to the one-plus-one collaboration with Michigan Tech, the college has developed its own program leading to the associate degree. The college also continues to participate in Fast Start for pre-college students interested in chemical-based career options. The 2000 Fast Start program was entirely underwritten by the Dow Corning Corporation.

Leveraged Funds

The National Science Foundation grant leveraged more than $60,000 from external partners, including Dow Chemical Company and Dow Corning Corporation. The additional funds supported a variety of activities:

- student internships
- Fast Start program at the university
- on-site training of recently hired employees
- mentors from business and industry
- travel and accommodations for project activities
- curriculum development and materials generation

What's Next?

The college put finishing touches on assessment and revision components of the program and assembled instructional materials in a format useful to other institutions. Upon request from other institutions, Delta will give advice on program equipment and training facilities, provide guidelines for faculty expertise to teach some of the more technically challenging courses, and offer advice on how to work with industrial partners. Efforts to improve the program will continue, especially in outreach efforts for student recruitment and retention.

Additional funding is being sought to help make available, at reasonable cost, the education and training outcomes achieved through the university's Process Simulation Center. Planning calls for the college to serve as the test site for the equipment and the faculty development instruction.

Fast Start students take necessary safety precautions prior to operating a 30-gallon polymerization reactor.

Other ideas include setting up a mechanism for evaluating process operators employed by both industrial partners so employees might gain some college credit for their experience. Many workers would like the opportunity to start or complete their associate degrees in process operations. The college offers some classes on the Internet and other distance learning approaches to individuals working shifts.

Materials Produced by the Program

Curricula, course descriptions, course outcomes, and objectives for the entire associate degree program in process operations are available to interested colleges. Additional information is also available.

Web sites at both institutions contain first- and second-year curricula, as well as the new technical chemistry courses at Delta College: www.delta.edu/~chm/chemproc.htm and www.delta.edu/~chm/chemproc2.htm.

Northwest Indian College Bellingham, Washington

Tribal Environmental and Natural Resource Management Degree Program [TENRM]

▶ **FOCUS**
▶ Environmental studies
▶ Tribal natural resource and environmental management
▶ Learning cohorts

College Environment

Higher education on the Lummi Reservation began with the establishment in 1971 of the Lummi Indian School of Aquaculture, a single-purpose institution designed to educate technicians for employment in Indian-owned and -operated fish and shellfish hatcheries throughout the United States and Canada. In the early 1980s, the employment demand for fishery technicians declined dramatically. At the same time, Lummi tribal leaders felt a need to focus tribal educational services on the education needs of Indians in Northwest Washington. On April 1, 1983, the Lummi Indian Business Council approved the charter for Lummi Community College. This charter established a public, non-profit, comprehensive community college for the purpose of providing postsecondary education services to the Native American communities in northwest Washington.

The name was changed to Northwest Indian College (NWIC) in January 1989 to reflect the college's mission more accurately. One of the college's primary goals is to develop the human resources of the Lummi Nation and other Northwest tribes. Northwest Indian College believes that self-awareness is the foundation that is necessary to build a career, to achieve a true sense of pride, and to cre-

Northwest Indian College
2522 Kwina Road
Bellingham, WA 98226
Ph: 360/676-2772
www.nwic.edu
President: Tommy H. Lewis, Jr.

Contact
Philip H. Duran, Principal Investigator
Science Department
Ph: 360/676-2772
Fax: 360/647-7084
E-mail: pduran@nwic.edu

Program Web Address
www.nwic.edu/programs/tenrm.html

ate a self-sufficient lifestyle. The college advances the idea that a self-awareness program must include a study of Indian culture, values, and history, and that appropriately supervised work experience builds confidence, esteem, and awareness.

Located between Seattle and Vancouver, British Columbia, Canada, on the Lummi Reservation near Bellingham, Washington, the college serves the various American Indian tribes of Washington, Idaho, and Oregon, although students come from other parts of North America. In addition to degree programs, it offers continuing education classes and course credits for students who are not pursuing a degree. Student enrollment varies from quarter to quarter, averaging about 1,300, of which 80 percent are Indian. The majority of students are women. Most of the faculty members are non-Indian.

The college is one of approximately 33 tribal colleges in the United States. It is a tribally controlled institution chartered by the Lummi Business Council and funded through the Bureau of Indian Affairs under Public Law 98-192. In 1994, the college became a land-grant college. A five-member board of trustees governs the college. Each trustee is a member of a participating Northwest Indian tribe and is appointed by the Lummi Indian Business Council.

NWIC offers an associate of arts and sciences (A.A.S.), an associate of technical arts (A.T.A.), a bachelor of arts in elementary education (the Native Teacher Preparation Program), and certificate programs as well as short-term training and workshops. Programs and courses focus on the needs of tribal communities. In addition to the main campus on the Lummi Nation, the college operates programs on more than 25 other reservations in the Northwest. Satellite-receiving classrooms operate on six reservations in Washington State.

Program Profile

Northwest Indian College is developing and testing a two-year associate of arts and sciences degree program in Native American environmental technology. The program is designed to meet a

I like the multidisciplinary aspect of this program. It keeps your mind challenged. We're re-learning things on a higher level. I think about how hard I've worked to get so far.
—Lummi student

critical need among area tribes to increase the number of Indians working in tribal natural resource and environmental management positions. The program has a strong tribal and cultural emphasis since these graduates must be able to walk in both worlds.

In addition to developing and testing a new curriculum, the program sponsors student internships and places students in work settings. The current grant, which expires August 31, 2000, provides funding for paid summer internships with the tribe. Internships are a graduation requirement. Some additional support comes from the college's foundation. College staff survey students to identify their interests before assigning internships. A second grant will allow the program to become self-sustaining.

A unique feature of the curriculum is the integration of economics, political science, Native American history, and science in large block classes. Rather than artificially dividing biology, economics, and English into separate courses, for example, a class on water will cover these subjects while studying fisheries, tribal law and regulation, tribal sovereignty, and economic development. In addition to academic and cultural integration, the same group of students go to class and work together as a learning community during the two-year program. This cohort approach provides a built-in support system as students help each other in study groups as well as with personal needs like transportation. It strives to build a close faculty team, trust between students and faculty, and honesty about the program's challenges.

Six 10-credit courses, representing six quarters of the curriculum, are organized as a coordinated studies program and team taught by faculty from

Biologist Dan Burns gives an introduction on the use of pipettes in the measurement of a volume metric flask.

It wasn't just the science that attracted me to this program; it was the combination of science and history.

—*Student*

Northwest Indian College and Western Washington University. To bring the real world into the classroom, tribal, industry, and government professionals in environmental technology periodically serve as lecturers. This specialized A.A.S. program meets all direct transfer agreements in the state.

Instructional methods are compatible with Native American learning styles. The methods include hands-on learning, an emphasis on speaking and writing skills, group projects, multidisciplinary courses, and internships. A Lummi professor at the college serves as "cultural consultant" to the non-Indian faculty and also provides an empathetic ear to students.

Three regional institutions collaborate with NWIC in these efforts: Huxley College and Fairhaven College, both at Western Washington University, and Evergreen State College. Each of these institutions has a track record of working effectively to meet the educational needs of Native American students and tribal communities. Mesa State College in Colorado and Diné Community College in Arizona also provided assistance to the college through their experience with their own advanced technological education grants from the National Science Foundation.

Why This Approach?

Two years before the National Science Foundation grant award, project staff conducted a needs survey of Tribal Council members and natural resource managers from 26 tribes in the Pacific Northwest. These tribal leaders identified a critical need for tribal managers and technicians in the resource management arena. Presently, non-Indians fill most professional positions in environmental protection and natural resource management within Pacific Northwest tribes. Indians in these positions do not always have the training needed to represent the best interests of the tribes. According to those surveyed, future employees need to have a strong background in science as well as a firm understanding of

PARTNERS

Western Washington University (WWU). Helped tailor the degree to make it compatible with transfer requirements and helped with student recruitment; provided publicity and student dormitory rooms. Faculty members serve on advisory committee.

Huxley College at WWU. Provided two teaching faculty and a dean for the advisory committee.

Fairhaven College at WWU. Faculty members serve on advisory committee.

Evergreen State College. Provided two faculty members for advisory committee and offered training in coordinated studies education.

Lummi Nation. Helped personalize the program to fit tribal needs and culture; provided meeting facilities and internship sites, guided field trips, and scholarships. Members serve on advisory committee.

U.S. Environmental Protection Agency. Provided scholarships; provided technical assistance and development of case studies. Agency personnel served on advisory committee.

U.S. Forest Service. Provided technical assistance. Service personnel serve on advisory committee.

Department of Energy. Provided student scholarships. Department personnel served on advisory committee.

Partnership for Environmental Technology Education (PETE). Provided student scholarships. Members served on advisory committee.

economics and political science. These leaders underscored the need for education program graduates to understand the role of culture in resource management. They also stated that the graduates must be well versed in Native American history and law, especially as these subjects relate to treaties, land allocation, jurisdiction, and sovereignty.

Major Achievements

Associate degree. Created a new degree program in tribal environmental and natural resource management that meets university transfer requirements. First cohort went through in June of 2000.

Retention. Two-thirds of the students who initially enrolled were still active in the program at the end of the first instructional year. Of the active students, 90 percent had completed more than half of the required credits in the first year. The credit completion rate was 73 percent for the cohort. During the summer of the second year, six students returned to finish incomplete work.

Articulation agreements. Finalized articulation agreements with partner institutions.

Scholarship program. Established a scholarship program that allows students to enroll in the program.

Outreach. Developed and distributed recruiting materials, including videos, brochures, press releases, and other handouts.

Team teaching. Organized a team teaching approach with faculty from Western Washington University.

Faculty development. Conducted faculty training programs that stressed the fundamentals of coordinated studies and learning communities. NWIC used a Lummi faculty member as key cultural advisor to the non-Indian faculty.

Influences on Program Development

The college tapped several sources for assistance in the development of its new degree program. Mesa State College provided curriculum materials and funds for cultural inclusion. Other support for curriculum materials came from the Center for Occupational Research and Development in Texas, the Northwest Center for Sustainable Resources in Oregon, and the Northwest Indian Fisheries Commission. The Northwest Indian College Foundation supported students with scholarship

Along with environmental issues, we covered areas of concern in tribal affairs... The most significant part of this program that makes it successful is the support we receive. This support is fundamental to our own values system.

—TENRM graduate

funds, sometimes on an emergency basis to help them stay in school. Faculty have helped students find transportation for the same reason.

Student Recruitment

In Indian country, student recruitment is often the most challenging task in the development of a postsecondary degree program. Although staff sent recruiting materials to prospective Indian students and advertised the program through radio and newspapers (including tribal sources), the most effective method was word of mouth. The most rewarding and effective activity was one in which staff set up a table with brochures and application packets in two local reservation stores. Community members who had been trained by program managers to talk about the program and the opportunities it presented managed the tables. Table monitors were given small stipends for their efforts. After only three days, this approach resulted in a dramatic increase in applicants.

The college's program brochure advertises its "integrated curriculum" and "collaborative learning"—both approaches appropriate to Native American learning styles. The publication also emphasizes phrases such as "hands-on learning," "strong tribal orientation," and "real world."

To recruit students, college faculty and staff went to the Lummi and other reservations, to powwows, and to other places where potential students might gather. They also conducted a telephone campaign and used the college's Web page to tell people about the new program and invite applicants. Students had to complete an application and provide letters of reference to be admitted into the program. All of the 16 students (male and female distributed fairly evenly) in the first cohort of the program were American Indians. Five came from reservations out-

I'm an enrolled member of the Jamul Reservation in California and was a Head Start teacher on the Rincon Reservation. Before that I cut trees. It wasn't just the science that attracted me to this program; it was the combination of science and history.

—*Student*

side Washington, including those in California and Alaska, and as far away as Maine. Washington State students represented 10 different tribes.

Unexpected Outcomes

The most significant unexpected outcome relates to student expectations. During the student interview process, all applicants indicated that they wanted to pursue a four-year degree. Originally, the program anticipated building two tracks: one for those wishing to complete only two years of study, and another for those wanting an A.A.S. degree for transfer to a four-year institution. As a result of the interview process, the program shifted its focus to the A.A.S. program.

The cohort model proved to be even more successful than anticipated. Students showed an exceptional acceptance of the group learning approach and adopted support groups as a way of life.

Most students, who needed to earn two credits in math each quarter, needed extra math. Each week, they took an extra hour of math called supplemental math, taught by one of the program faculty. Students themselves helped organize informal tutoring sessions.

Recognition

- TENRM is featured in "Tribal Program Focuses on Learning Styles," *Window on Western* magazine, Western Washington University, Spring 1999.
- Two TENRM graduates gave presentations at the 8th International Symposium on Society and Resource

Management, a professional meeting held at Western Washington University, June 17-22, 2000. A separate TENRM session was also presented at the same conference.
- Four TENRM student graduates received scholarships for further study, including Gates, Morris Udall, and Packard scholarships.

College Commitment

In addition to giving strong philosophical support to the program, the college provided funds for equipment and donated the time of the college recruiter to bring students to the new curriculum.

The college is committed to continuing the program beyond the current grant period and has created a full-time faculty position for TENRM student recruitment, development, and retention. This position will help reduce faculty time requirements as the program becomes self-sustaining during the next three-year grant period.

Leveraged Funds

Employers provided $36,000 for student internships. Each of the collaborating institutions and organizations also committed significant resources to the program, including dorm rooms, use of meeting facilities, guided field trips, and additional support for student scholarships.

TENRM students participate in an Introduction to Chemistry lab and use a volume metric flask, graduated cylinders, pipettes, and graduated beakers. The experiment involves measuring the accuracy of the equipment listed above with an introduction to the concept of human error.

What's Next?

The curriculum will be a standing part of the education program offered by the college. Institutionalization was built into the effort from its inception. Initially, the new curriculum was to be offered only at the main campus, but plans are underway to broaden the offerings through distance learning and at remote sites. Although the cohort approach to teaching and learning is very time-consuming for faculty, the college is looking toward applying it and the team-teaching approach in other courses not presently a part of the program. The college also plans to create third- and fourth-year courses to form a bachelor's degree program. A second cohort began in the fall of 2000. Beginning in 2001, two cohorts will be studying simultaneously. In an effort to create a self-sustained program, the college is seeking additional partnership agreements.

Materials Produced by the Program

In addition to the curriculum itself, Northwest Indian College developed two brochures to market the program. "Tribal Environmental and Natural Resource Management" contains details on the program design and descriptions of courses and credit analysis. "To Be the Eagle's View" provides an overview of environmental studies.

During the fall of 2000, an informative and practical curriculum package designed to assist faculty desiring to start a similar program at their institutions will be distributed to all tribal colleges. The package will consist of a video and curriculum planning guide.

Curriculum outlines for six 10-credit courses, which comprise 60 of the 90 required credits of the associate degree, are shown below. Students admitted into the program take one large block course and one 3-credit course each quarter. Students will also complete a paid internship in either their first or second quarter.

TRIBAL ENVIRONMENTAL AND NATURAL RESOURCE MANAGEMENT DEGREE PROGRAM

Course 1	To Be the Eagle's View
Goals	Excite students and help them see how this program relates to their community and themselves
	Help them establish a connection with the land, ocean, and water (Whatcom County)
	Bring their basic skills up to the level required
	Time to form relationships with other students and faculty
Themes	"In the beginning..." (creation stories)
	Evolutionary theory
	Stewardship
	"All things are connected"
Knowledge/Skills Emphasized	Basic writing (journal writing)
	Biology/Ecology/Native American (NA) philosophy
Other Knowledge/Skills	Basics of chemistry
	Basic geology
Integrated Course Credits	Native American History (SS2)
	Introduction to Biology (Biol. 101) (2)
	Introduction to Computers (CMPS 101) (2)
	Geology (2)

Separate Courses	Intro. to Successful Learning (4) for both A.A.S. and A.T.A. tracks
External Assistance	Geologist

Course 2 — Water

Goals	Cultural and economic importance of water (myth, treaties) Understanding of the hydrological cycle and human effects Understanding of aquatic ecosystems (river, lake, wetland) Basic water quality knowledge and analysis Learning to work in teams (first group project)
Themes	Cultural/economic importance of water: its connection to treaties, law, regulation, and jurisdiction Water connecting ocean, freshwater, and land Case study: Whatcom County water conflicts
Knowledge/Skills Emphasized	Human use of and effect on hydrological cycle American political system: law, policy, and regulation
Other Knowledge/Skills	Applied use of math Hydropower Wastewater treatment Team dynamics, conflict resolution
Integrated Course Credits	Native American (2-SS1,OT1) Political Science (3) Speech (1) Computers (1) Biology (2) Chemistry (1 OT)
Separate Courses	Humanities (3) for A.A.S. track Technical (3) for A.T.A. track

Course 3 — Land

Goals	Cultural and economic importance of land: treaties and sovereignty Understanding of human use of land: economics and practices
Themes	Pacific Northwest reservation forests and forestry Agricultural impacts on reservations: income and effects

Knowledge/Skills Emphasized	Federal Indian Policy: treaty rights, sovereignty, jurisdiction Forests and forestry Agriculture Microeconomics
Other Knowledge/Skills	Soils and geology Mapping, GIS/GPS, remote sensing Solid and hazardous wastes: toxicology
Integrated Course Credits	Math 102 (2) Economics (2) Political Science (Amer. and Tribal) (1) Geography (2) Geology (3)
Separate Courses	Humanities (3) for A.A.S. track Technical (3) for A.T.A. track
External Assistance	Geologist Economist

Course 4	**Ocean**
Goals	Understanding of the cultural/economic importance of fishing to Pacific Northwest Tribes Understanding of biological and chemical processes at play in the ocean Basic use of basic math in description and problem solving Further improvement of writing skills (descriptive, analytical, comparative/contrastive)
Themes	Fishing: ancestors to present time Food webs, limiting factors, and population dynamics
Knowledge/Skills Emphasized	Fishing history, economics, treaties, practices, etc. Basic chemistry Writing skills Marine botany and zoology: life cycles, food webs
Other Knowledge/Skills	Bolt decision, Law of the Sea Use of computers in modeling and harvest management Shoreline processes (erosion) Chart reading
Integrated Course Credits	English 101 (2) Native American History (SS2) Chemistry (2) Biology (1) Math (2) Speech (1)

| Separate Courses | Humanities (3) for A.A.S. track |
| | Technical (3) for A.T.A. track |

Course 5 — Making Connections, Finding Balance

Goals	Understanding the connections between cultural needs, economic development, and environmental protection
	Knowing the types of information needed and steps required to do an analysis
	Understanding the types of analyses that are carried out
	Learning how to prepare and defend a project proposal
	Learning how to work in teams
	Ability to complete a formal project proposal

| Themes | Reservation case studies: finding the balance |
| | Preparation of a project proposal |

Knowledge/Skills Emphasized	Technical/argumentative/grant writing
	Economic analysis
	Watershed analysis
	Tribal political organization/operation

Other Knowledge/Skills	Budgeting
	Supervision
	Introduction to EIS

Integrated Course Credits	English (3)
	Economics (3)
	Statistics (2)
	Political Science (2)

| Separate Courses | Humanities (3) for A.A.S. track |
| | Technical (3) for A.T.A. track |

| External Assistance | Economist |

Course 6 — Bring It Together (Project)

| | Capstone project (proposal prepared in course 5) |

| Goals | Ability to work in teams to complete a field project |
| | Ability to write and present a technical report |

| Themes | Field/lab/library research of economic and environmental impact |

| Knowledge/Skills Emphasized | Data collection (field, lab, and library) |
| | Technical writing |

	Environmental/economic impact analysis Team dynamics Speech
Other Knowledge/ Skills	Job skills (resume writing, job search, etc.) Statistics
Integrated Course Credits	Speech (2) English (5) Statistics (1) Independent study (2) (selects area related to project)
Separate Courses	Humanities (3) for A.A.S. track Technical (3) for A.T.A. track
Other Faculty	All faculty to mentor one project group

Summer Internship (to be completed 1st or 2nd summer)

Goals	Placement of a student in order to gain job-related and technical skills To write a summary report of summer project or experience
Knowledge/ Skills Emphasized	Job skills Report writing Technical skills

Course 11 credits (classified as technical)

NOTE: The college acknowledges the important contributions to this program made by Gigi Berardi, Dan Burns, Roberto Gonzales-Plaza, Lynn Robbins, Ted Williams, and Wayne Woods.

Pima Community College
Tucson, Arizona

Teamed Internships: Innovative Education for Environmental Technicians and Engineers

▶ **FOCUS**
▶ Paid internships
▶ Two-person teams representing community college technicians and university engineers

College Environment

Pima Community College (PCC) is situated in Tucson, traditionally considered a retirement community without major industry. The University of Arizona is Tucson's largest employer, followed by the State of Arizona and Davis Monthan Air Force Base. Tucson's largest private employer, and fourth largest employer overall, is Raytheon Systems Company (formerly Hughes Missile Systems). Other employers include optics and mining companies and many small environmental firms with 6 to 100 employees. These environmental firms work in the areas of environmental consulting, soil remediation, and water and wastewater treatment, among other enterprises.

The population of Pima County is expected to continue to grow rapidly from its 1997 level of 805,100 to more than 1,000,000 by 2010. The county's minority population is 24.5 percent Hispanic, 2.9 percent African American, 2.6 percent Native American, and 1.7 percent Asian/ Pacific Islander. However, the percentage of minorities in professional fields is low and has remained relatively constant at only 3 to 5 percent.

Pima Community College serves residents of Pima and Santa Cruz counties in southern Arizona.

Pima County Community College District
8181 East Irvington Road
Tucson, AZ 85709-4000
Ph: 520/206-7000
www.pima.edu
District Chancellor: Robert C. Jensen

Contacts
Greg Ogden, Principal Investigator
Pima Community College
Ph: 520/206-7692
Fax: 520/206-7622
E-mail: gogden@pimacc.pima.edu

Kimberly Ogden, Co-principal Investigator
University of Arizona
Ph: 520/621-9484
Fax: 520/621-6048
E-mail: ogden@erc.arizona.edu

Jennifer Croissant, Co-principal Investigator
University of Arizona
Ph: 520/626-7110
Fax: 520/621-8059
E-mail: jlc@u.arizona.edu

The college's first classes met in the fall of 1969 at Tucson Medical Center, Villa Maria, and Marana. In the fall of 1970, Pima College officially opened its doors to 3,543 students. Classes were held in the unlikely quarters of a hangar at the Tucson

International Airport. Today the college enrolls more than 65,000 credit and non-credit students annually. Its five campuses offer university transfer programs, occupational and developmental education, and general studies courses. Additional classes, workshops, and seminars are held at more than 100 off-campus locations in Tucson, Green Valley, and Nogales, Arizona.

The college's Community Campus provides televised classes on local cable channels that apply toward a student's degree and that can be transferred to another college or university. The Corporate and Community Education office offers customized training for the business community.

The student population at PCC is diverse. Approximately 55 percent of the students are women, 28 percent Hispanic, 4 percent African American, 4 percent Asian American, and 3 percent Native American. Full-time equivalent students number more than 16,000. The average age of PCC students is 28. Sixty-one percent are not intending to transfer to a four-year institution; 26 percent attend full-time. PCC enrollment includes more than 600 international students from 80 countries.

Laura Lawson and Angela Murphy work together on a computer spreadsheet for a waste management project as part of their summer internship at Hughes Missile Systems (now Raytheon Systems Company), Tucson, Arizona.

There has got to be a little more give and take [in a team environment] and [an understanding] that not everybody is always right.
—Student comment after internship

The University of Arizona is a student-centered research university that is ranked in the top 15 nationwide for total research dollars. There are currently about 34,000 students enrolled in the university, from all 50 states and about 110 foreign countries. Approximately one-fourth of all freshmen are from minority groups. Many of the 1,600 faculty are recognized internationally in their specialties and are members of national professional academies.

Program Profile

The ATE program in environmental technology and engineering is a collaborative effort among Pima Community College, the University of Arizona, regional industries, federal research facilities, and secondary schools in the Tucson metropolitan area. The major goal is to address the perceived differences and tensions between technicians and engineers through the creation of challenging industrial and research internships for environmental technology and engineering student teams. The project strives to instill the importance of lifelong learning and equip students with the interpersonal, technical, and communication skills necessary to succeed in the continuously evolving field of environmental technology. It is designed to bridge the gap between technicians and engineers in order to facilitate smooth introductions of new technologies and foster teamwork between operations and management.

Firms volunteer to manage the intern teams, participate on the project advisory committee, and assess intern performance. Team members are responsible for making presentations to local high school teachers and students on the career potential of environmental technology and engineering. In the summer, the interns and project principals present lab experiment demonstrations to high school teachers during a three-day institute held on the community college campus. As part of this institute, the teachers also tour research laboratories in the area.

One team, working with WEST, Inc., optimized a copper-ore precipitation process. The project involved determining the optimal dosage of a proprietary coagulant that would minimize ore loss. Implementation of this process by WEST's client is expected to result in savings exceeding $1 million per year. The team was also instrumental in the testing and verification of a novel scale inhibitor. Another team working with Raytheon Missile Systems successfully optimized a metal waste pretreatment process resulting in the elimination of a costly flocculent polymer and the savings of tens of thousands of dollars.

—Student comment after intern experience

PARTNERS

The industrial sponsors listed below provided internships for the Pima Community College and University of Arizona students. Each company assigns an official to participate on the project advisory committee.

WEST, Inc.

Los Alamos National Laboratory

Tucson Electric Power

Raytheon Missile Systems

City of Tucson, Office of Environmental Management

Calgon Carbon Oxidation*

Zenitech*

*Calgon Carbon and Zenitech left Tucson following the first year of the internship program.

The program emphasizes communication, teamwork, and group problem solving. To give students real-world experience, it includes external constraints such as cost and timeliness, quality, social and environmental concerns, health and safety, and other elements. The program underscores the benefits of multicultural diversity. Thus far, it has supported five technician/engineer intern teams. Assigned to a local firm for two semesters and a summer session, each team averaged 20 hours per week at the business site.

Why This Approach?

The program addresses the perceived and ideological differences between technicians and engineers. The majority of technicians in today's industry are involved with day-to-day operations, while engineers typically are responsible for plant management. The fundamental differences between operations and management—coupled with variations in educational backgrounds and experiences—create an artificial barrier to efficient plant upgrades and modernization. Typically, both engineers and technicians are responsible for these barriers, whether

they arise from young, inexperienced engineers proposing impractical or infeasible modifications because they "work on paper" or from operators' resisting change, preferring the "way it has always been done."

In addition to these perceived differences between engineers and technicians, traditional engineering and science education is lacking in some aspects. In particular, industry people report that students lack a holistic view of their work and are unable to communicate effectively with peers and supervisors, work effectively in teams, and are unaware of the work environment and employer expectations. For example, students often have had little exposure to the diversity of cultures in the workplace. They also have little understanding of the environmental life cycle (from raw materials to the waste product), engineering and science as an integral part of societal change, or the interconnection between society and all the disciplines of science and engineering. Employer focus groups have indicated that many environmental technology

MAJOR ACHIEVEMENTS

Education-industry partnership. Key players created an effective network, including local industry, the University of Arizona, Pima Community College, Tucson Unified School District, and other area high schools.

Internships. Student interns developed laboratory experiments for courses at the University of Arizona and Pima Community College.

High school outreach. Interns made presentations to local area high school science classes.

Conference. The principal investigators developed and conducted a high school teacher science and mathematics conference.

Diversity. Seventy-five percent of the 14 students who participated during the second year of the project were from underrepresented and minority groups.

Industrial support. New industrial sponsors were added after the program began.

Employment. Student interns received job offers from industrial sponsors.

College student impact. The program indirectly affected more than 150 environmental science technician and undergraduate engineering students through teacher training and curriculum development activities.

I gained experience in equipment construction. One of the most important things I gained was experience with working with other people of different educational levels and expectations. It was interesting to see the different opinions on how to design and construct our testing chamber between the engineering supervisor at Calgon and the head technician. It gave me good insight on how to approach and motivate people as well as how to find the middle ground between the perfect design that is impossible to build and the "fly-by-the-seat-of-your-pants" approach that is constructible but doesn't function for the original intentions.

—Student comment after an internship

concentrated on engineering sciences and the understanding of fundamental phenomena.

This grant program begins to address these issues by having students work in teams, prepare and make presentations, and gain real world experiences in the environmental field. The student teams develop hands-on experiments and demonstrations that are used in chemical engineering and environmental technician classes. The student teams also disseminate these experiments during high school outreach activities.

Influences on Program Development

To get the teamed internship program off the ground, college staff relied on existing literature on teaching and engineering education, their own personal experiences, and experience of business partners. They recalled some of the conflicts between technicians and engineers, newcomers and old-timers. Safety was sometime an issue (e.g., why an oldtimer should wear gloves when for years he'd used his bare hands to clean his equipment). Local industrial sponsors offered insights into the need for enhanced teamwork. Some had problems with

graduates lack technical expertise, have weak scientific skills, and lack critical thinking skills. Pima's ATE program addresses these issues head-on.

To be competitive in today's global marketplace, technicians and engineers must have effective communication skills, a sense of the total business equation, and the ability to define problems and consider alternative solutions. To meet these challenges, both four-year and two-year educational institutions must revise their teaching methods. No longer satisfactory is the engineering education philosophy practiced over the past four decades that

[High school outreach presentations] should definitely be on the list of things to do again. Dreaded it at first, but liked it in the end.
— *College student*

young "booksmart" engineers coming into a plant and trying to "change the world" without working with the technicians. The techs, on the other hand, were often unwilling to learn new systems or ways of operating to improve things.

Student Recruitment

Student interns and seminar students are recruited through fliers distributed to all sophomore and junior chemical and environmental engineering classes at the university and to all environmental science classes at the college's East Campus. Informational posters and flyers distributed to the science departments at Pima's four other campuses helped recruit additional students. Intern team presentations to local high school science and chemistry classes also served as a recruiting approach.

Unexpected Outcomes

Several enhancements in Pima Community College's academic program resulted from the ATE program. Through increased interaction and networking with local industries, the college's Department of Environmental Sciences has been able to diversify its industrial advisory board. Increased awareness by university faculty and an increased presence of Pima faculty at the University of Arizona have improved Pima's new degree transfer program. In this program, technician students earning an associate of arts degree for transfer in environmental science now transfer directly into a bachelor's degree program in the Department of Environmental Sciences at the university.

Technician interns from Pima observed that regional employers were more interested in hiring

We view our participation in the internship program as part of our corporate social responsibility.
— *Company official*

Pima's environmental technician graduates than the environmental science bachelor's degree graduates from the state universities because Pima's students are equipped with OSHA 40 (Hazwopper) certificates. PCC is receiving more calls from university students seeking OSHA 40 training.

Educating local industry about the advantages of providing paid internship opportunities for technician interns is a very slow process, and the initial response from many potential sponsors is still negative. However, many of those who have become industrial sponsors have made full-time job offers to the students following their internships.

This program has encouraged many technician students to transfer to the University of Arizona to obtain bachelor of science degrees. University students have expressed interest in continuing their studies beyond the baccalaureate degree. Overall, the student teams have forged tight bonds between students at both institutions that have continued past graduation.

Perhaps most important of all, employers have begun to view themselves as integral parts of the education system.

Recognition

Pima Community College's environmental technology and engineering program has garnered recognition through the active involvement of program staff in conferences and other meetings.

Among them are the national conferences of the American Institute for Chemical Engineers and the American Society for Engineering Education. The principal investigator also presented at the

Ellen Kitchen (UA) assists John Zumbrunnen (PCC) with his SCBA during OSHA 40 Hazwopper training.

Interns are valuable assets to our company because they don't cost us much and they make important contributions to our work.

—Company official

national ATE conference co-sponsored by the National Science Foundation and the American Association of Community Colleges. Regionally, the program was showcased at the annual Western Partners in Environmental Technology Education (PETE) conference.

At the local level, program staff presented materials generated by the grant and provided reviews of the project to other community college and university faculty as well as to high school teachers. These activities included presentations at the eighth Annual Science & Mathematics Conference held in February 1998 at the Biosphere, the Maricopa Community College All Faculty Convocation, and an NSF Regional Workshop in December 1997.

Additional papers were prepared for the *Journal of Engineering Education* and the *ATEEC News,* sponsored by the Advanced Technological Education Environmental Center.

College Commitment

Both Pima Community College and the University of Arizona have made strong commitments to this project to ensure success. The college's commitments include release time for the principal investigator and travel funds for program faculty and student interns to attend annual AACC/ATE conferences, regional workshops, and outreach presentations. Pima's East Campus hosted the 1998 Summer High School Mathematics and Science Conference, providing laboratory and lecture facilities and catered lunches for the two-day event. During the past two years, the college's Arizona State Environmental Technology Training Center also provided OSHA 40 (Hazwopper) training seminars, at significantly reduced rates, for project participants.

The University of Arizona's involvement with the project includes faculty release time for the co-principal investigators. In addition, the university offered substantial mentoring and guidance by fac-

ulty and staff from its Department of Chemical and Environmental Engineering for academic research projects offered to intern participants. The department secured $10,000 for equipment and laboratory curriculum upgrades for this project. The department's NSF/Environmental Research Center for Benign Semiconductor Manufacturing co-hosted the Summer High School Teacher Conference.

Leveraged Funds

Corporate partners supported Pima's ATE program through cash and other donations. Project faculties were able to make use of $10,000 in matching funds provided by Hughes Missile Systems. These funds were used in developing an undergraduate combustion laboratory experiment at the university and to enhance a water/wastewater clarifier demonstration model built for Pima's environmental sciences program. Tucson Electric Power fully funded an additional intern team at their offices, a value of $12,000. Solar Store donated several thousand dollars worth of equipment to the East Campus of the community college for a Koe-pond, including a photovoltaic array, battery storage, and a circulating pump.

What's Next?

College leaders and staff continue to work with local industry to coordinate paid internships and co-ops for technician and engineering students. In an effort to enhance student advising and encourage participation in science and engineering career paths, the college continues to offer the high school teacher conferences nationally to inform teachers and counselors about the differences between engineers and technicians. The conferences share with other institutions the laboratory experiments and educational modules developed through the program.

Materials Produced by the Program

Student interns have developed laboratory experiments and demonstrations that are available to all PCC faculty. The experiments include a colorimetric test for qualitative determination of phosphates in water samples and a personal protective-equipment experiment examining the chemical compatibility of various glove materials. Small, simple versions of these laboratory experiments were disseminated to teachers at the summer High School Teacher Conference. The interns also developed laboratory experiments and components that are integrated into the chemical engineering junior- and senior-year curricula at the university. These materials are available from the principal investigator.

References

Black, K. M. 1994. An industry view of engineering education. *Journal of Engineering Education*: 26-28.

Bordogna, J., E. Fromm, and E. Ernst. 1993. Engineering education: Innovation through integration. *Journal of Engineering Education*: 3-8.

Katz, S.M. 1993. The entry-level engineer: Problems in transition from student to professional. *Journal of Engineering Education*: 171-174.

O'Reilly, D., J. Deegan, and L. Colombo. 1995. *Environmental studies 2000: An overview of undergraduate interdisciplinary environmental programs and the careers of their graduates.* Boston: Environmental Careers Organization.

Prados, J. W. 1995. Engineering education reform: The NSF role. Presentation at the 1995 AIChE Annual Meeting, November, Miami.

Tau, B. Y. 1993. Senior/sophomore co-class instruction: Teaching interpersonal management skills in engineering. *Journal of Engineering Education*: 126-129.

Queensborough Community College New York, New York

Technology Instruction for the 21st Century: Phase II Telecommunications

▶ **FOCUS**
▶ Advanced telecommunications technology for improved teaching and learning
▶ Telecommunications courses and curriculum development
▶ Internet-based curriculum modules
▶ Faculty development workshops

College Environment

Serving the Borough of Queens in New York, Queensborough Community College (QCC) serves a diverse area, where foreign-born individuals head nearly half of all households. Significant increases in the number of Hispanics and Asians occurred since 1990. The college's service area does not have a single dominant employer in terms of number of employees, but several employment entities are dominant: banking, Wall Street, and other financial services, and telecommunications. Consolidated Edison (the local power company) has a significant employment presence, but its employment base decreased in recent years. Verizon (formerly Bell Atlantic) is a major employer.

Part of the City University of New York, QCC offers associate degree and certificate programs that prepare its students for transfer to four-year institutions and for entry into the job market. The college functions as a community resource by serving the educational, professional, and cultural needs of the general community. It also engages in active outreach activities that invite members of the business, labor, and industrial communities to participate in special programs and events. Its 34-acre campus is located in the suburban-like community of Bayside, Queens.

Queensborough Community College
56th and Springfield Boulevard
New York, NY 11364
Ph: 718/631-6262
www.qcc.cuny.edu
President: Eduardo Marti

Contacts
Bernard E. Mohr
Professor, Electrical and Computer Engineering Technology
Queensborough Community College
Ph: 718/631-6207
Fax: 718/357-4564
E-mail: bemohr@delphi.com

Russell K. Hotzler
University Dean of Academic Affairs
City University of New York
Ph: 212/794-5469
Fax: 212/794-5690
E-mail: RKHBH@cunyvm.cuny.edu

Program Web Address
www.ecet.qcc.cuny.edu

Ten major buildings are used for instruction and extracurricular activities.

Day and evening divisions serve 10,355 students, with daytime students representing 85 percent of the total enrollment. The electrical and computer engineering technology department has more than 750 students enrolled, with about half in computer engineering technology and the rest fairly evenly divided between electrical engineering technology and telecommunications programs. The department is the largest engineering technology program in New York State.

The college recruits approximately 88 percent of its students from the Borough of Queens and nearly all students (90 percent) are enrolled in degree programs. Student enrollment overall is 20.4 percent African American, 19.3 percent Hispanic, 15.5 percent Asian, 0.15 percent Native American, and 6.4 percent "other students;" 9.6 percent are classified as unknown. The student body represents 115 countries of origin.

Unlike many other community colleges, men (56.3 percent) outnumber women. Students range in age from 15 to 86 years old, but about 36 percent of the entering freshman are 19 years old or younger. The trend is toward greater numbers of students over 25 years of age. Full-time and part-time student distributions are 55.5 percent and 44.5 percent. Fourteen percent of the students participate in the English as a second language program. Nearly one-third of the students hold full-time jobs. Family incomes are generally low—one-third of the students are from families with annual incomes below $20,000. Entering students must take a placement examination to determine their levels of reading, writing, and mathematical skills. About 75 percent of entering students must take a developmental reading course, 55 percent a writing course, and 85 percent a mathematics course.

A. Svetlana Koyenova pondering data in Queensborough Community College's first NSF-funded laboratory.

It's great! It's new and innovative. Its easier, friendly, and fun to do.
—Student

Program Profile

The college is completing the second of a planned three-phase program to engineer major improvements in its technology programs and teaching methods. Using telecommunications technologies as a vehicle for instructional change, Phase II integrates four components: curriculum and instructional materials development, instrumentation and laboratory improvement, faculty enhancement and dissemination of instructional materials, and distance learning and remote access technology. The goal is to provide science and technology students with more marketable skills, develop methods to keep curricula in step with cutting-edge technology, and to promote activities that significantly improve faculty skills.

As part of the ATE program, the college designed and installed two telecommunications laboratories to accommodate the five core telecommunications courses:

- analog and telephony telecommunications
- digital and data communications
- local area networks
- advanced topics in telecommunications
- computer applications in telecommunications

Local and distributed networks are taught in one laboratory, while analog and telephony communications are taught in the second.

Faculty developed courseware modules that may be used in the five core courses. Authoring for the modules was done in Authorware, ToolBook, or Visual Basic, depending on course requirements. Courseware was designed for stand-alone computers, then for Intranet delivery, and finally for Internet delivery. The plan is to have all courseware converted to Internet formats for more effective dissemination. Newly created materials include networked laboratory manuals, text, and student exercises. They are available in a small modular format to facilitate their incorporation into technology education courses at

I think we should use more online lab and forget the [text] book.

—*Student*

other institutions and for easy use on the internet. Module topics include local and wide area networks (LANs and WANs) and analog and digital communications.

To disseminate products completed in the project and to help faculty learn to author effective multimedia-based materials, QCC offered six one-week summer workshops, two each year over a three-year period. Increasing numbers of people applied each summer, testifying to the great need for workshops such as these.

Why This Approach?

Traditional approaches to instructional improvement have attempted simply to overlay existing laboratory and classroom lessons with new commercial technology and to migrate to upgraded platforms, such as better operating systems or faster video displays. These methods have not proven very effective in providing students with the skills needed to master the technology. During periods of rapid technological change, such methods have incurred unmanageable costs. At the same time, shifts in global economics and declines in national defense spending have altered regional employment opportunities and practices. This is especially true in the New York metropolitan area, where the demand for technicians in manufacturing and aerospace industries has virtually disappeared. According to an article in the *New York Times*, "Manufacturing that remains in the New York region is heavily devoted to the local market while its cutting-edge services—finance, law, communications, popular culture, and medicine—are increasingly in demand throughout the global economy" (Redburn 1994). Telecommunication technologies are creating new employment opportunities in these global services, and technicians will prove to be the infrastructure of technical enterprises.

In spite of these trends, Queensborough recognized that there will be a shortage of qualified candidates to enter and successfully complete science and engineering technology programs unless

PARTNERS

Verizon, Northeast Center for Telecommunications Technology, and New York State Consortium. Helped develop an associate degree program that will ensure a technical workforce positioned to address the competitive requirements of the telecommunications industry.

Consortium for minority participation. City College/CUNY, New York (lead college); LaGuardia Community College, New York; Medgar Evers College, New York; Queensborough Community College, New York; York College, Pennsylvania; and New York City high schools, including Washington High School and A. Philip Randolph High School. In developing the network infrastructure and Internet access, Queensborough program staff joined a CUNY-Alliance for Minority Participation/NASA-Goddard cooperative venture to secure grant support from NASA for an initiative titled "An Urban Collaboration for Network Connectivity and Internet Access" (Minority University Space Interdisciplinary Network—MU-SPIN). This effort resulted in a $2.5 million, five-year award to enhance the research and educational opportunities available to minority students.

instructional methods become more effective. The college's experience confirmed these concerns. It faced declining enrollments in science, mathematics, and technology, and students were less prepared and committed to academic tasks. Retention and graduation were also lower, and fewer students transferred to baccalaureate science and engineering programs. At the same time, community college faculty struggled with infusing new technology into their curricula because of high instructional workloads, lack of funding to support revision, and apprehension over learning new technology. The ATE program came along at the right time to help overcome these challenges.

Influences on Program Development

The college took advantage of a number of sources in developing their ATE program. QCC worked with Bell Atlantic, the ATE Northeast Center for Telecommunications Technology at

MAJOR ACHIEVEMENTS

Telecommunications laboratories
Telecommunications Lab Area 1: Local and Distributed Systems—developed to train students in a variety of digital telecommunications specialties, from local area networks to distributed information systems, including bridged local networks, wide area networks, virtual networks, and Internet works.

Telecommunications Lab Area 2: Analog and Telephony Communications and Fiber Optic Technology—developed to teach telecommunications fundamentals, including analog and data communications, telephony, and fiber optics technology.

Degree programs: Associate in Applied Science in Telecommunications
Corporate-specific A.A.S. in telecommunications (60 credits) for Verizon employees participating in the Next Step retraining program.

A.A.S. degree program in telecommunications (68-69 credits) designed to be TAC/ABET accredited.

Telecommunications courseware. Developed courseware for teaching analog, digital, and network communications; currently used by students and instructors in telecommunications courses.

Faculty development workshops. Presented six NSF Undergraduate Faculty Enhancement workshops to 64 participants from across the United States and Puerto Rico. Visitors have come from Japan and the Netherlands to audit and observe the workshops.

Springfield Technical Community College in Massachusetts, and a New York State consortium to develop an associate degree program in telecommunications. Committee members designed the course content and laboratory experiments at consortia meetings.

Since many telecommunications skills may be classified as information technology (IT) skills, the program used IT skills standards defined by the ATE-supported NorthWest Center for Emerging

I would like to measure all values using computers and update information from that to the data table and graph.

—*Student*

Technologies at Bellevue Community College in Washington. Those skills were developed in cooperation with the Regional Advanced Technology Education Consortium, the Washington State Board for Community and Technical Colleges, the Washington Software and Digital Media Alliance, and the Society for Information Management. These skills, defined in *Building a Foundation for Tomorrow: Skills Standards for Information Technology*, reflect an industry-wide consensus of IT industry professionals. These are measurable competency-based skills that incorporate foundation skills and IT workplace competencies that include technical knowledge and performance criteria. Foundation skills are broad-based workplace categories defined by the U.S. Department of Labor in its SCANS (Secretary's Commission on Achieving Necessary Skills) report.

Prior to the college's NSF ATE grants, the work supported by other funding sources—including NSF Instrumentation and Laboratory Improvement and NSF Course and Curriculum Development—helped jumpstart the college's efforts. Federal vocational education funds through the Carl D. Perkins Vocational and Applied Technology Education Act also assisted the college in redirecting its technology programs.

Student Recruitment
The college recruits students through connections with local high schools. Staff contact career counselors and academic advisors, especially in the Borough of Queens, to tell them about QCC's program through brochures and presentations to potential students. Members of the college's Electrical and Computer Engineering Technology Department also visit technical high schools.

Unexpected Outcomes
A significant outcome came from a surprise partnership with Verizon. The college reshaped its A.A.S. degree program in telecommunications to suit the

The students liked the presentation courseware because the lecture became "alive." The instructor can go through each topic of the laboratory experiment and demonstrate to the student what actually [will happen at the] workbench. The student is now better prepared.

—Instructor

specific requirements of Verizon's Next Steps program, a company-wide effort to expand the skills and knowledge of its employees. The partnership was triggered by a contact the company made at the National Science Foundation.

In addition, the college experienced extraordinary success with its modules and technology integration. The development of Web-based instrumentation courseware far exceeded the original goal. The college now delivers two electronics courses online.

Recognition

The project and its principal investigator received recognition at the City University Chancellor's 1998 Convocation honoring faculty for their contributions to the university. Program staff produced many publications and presented at several conferences, including the Education Technology Conference, the League for Innovation in the Community College Conference on Information Technology, and ATE conferences co-sponsored by NSF and the American Association of Community Colleges. Topics included electronics laboratory instruction, creating multimedia and Internet courseware, school and business partnerships, and interactive Web-based lab experiments.

Instructors from across the country participate in Queensborough Community College's Undergraduate Faculty Enhancement Workshops, including the following:

Technology Instruction for the 21st Century: Process and Products (two five-day multimedia workshops)

Creating Multimedia and Internet Courseware with ToolBook II (three-day NSF Chautauqua short course, sponsored by the University of Puerto Rico and the NSF Alliance for Minority Participation)

Practical Techniques for the Development of Computer Assisted Multimedia Educational Modules Using Authorware Professional for Windows (three-day workshop sponsored by the NSF Alliance for Minority Participation of Puerto Rico)

Engineering Technology Instruction for the 21st Century: Process and Products (three-day workshop for New York State faculty participating in the NYNEX (later Bell Atlantic) Next Step program)

Engineering Technology Instruction for the 21st Century: Process and Products (three-day multimedia workshop for national faculty, sponsored by NSF)

College Commitment

The ATE program enjoys strong administrative support from the college president as well as the dean of academic affairs, who served as a co-principal investigator. Additional support comes from college funds and a commitment to obtaining continuation funds for the program's Phase III, Information Technology.

Bruce Naples (co-principal investigator) instructing students in the telecommunications lab.

Leveraged Funds

Queensborough's ATE program generated additional funds within the college and beyond. In addition to the matching funds, the college provided nearly $40,000 for telecommunications laboratory equipment. The linkage with NASA and its MU-SPIN initiative provided more than $200,000 to support the project's courseware development and dissemination objectives. ELANIX Corporation donated $3,500 in software—16 site licenses for SystemView—that students and faculty used in telecommunications courses.

What's Next?

Project staff hope to build on Phases I and II and follow up with a third phase focusing on information technology. This would offer students greater employment opportunities, further develop the best practices of this project, and accommodate even more faculty in courseware development workshops.

Materials Produced by the Program

Curriculum and instructional materials developed in the preceding ATE project—Technology Instruction for the 21st Century: Phase I—are part of the core curriculum for the A.A.S. degree in the telecommunications technology program for Bell Atlantic employees. Phase II continues this initiative by providing more advanced courseware in telecommunications and networking. Instructional Web-based courseware is accessible via the college's Web server at www.ecet.qcc.cuny.edu.

As part of the project, each summer 32 faculty from across the United States participate in Undergraduate Faculty Enhancement Workshops. Participants receive workshop instructional materials and develop multimedia and Internet courseware prototypes. Each session produces a compact disk that contains workshop instructional prototypes and other project courseware. It is available from the college.

References

NorthWest Center for Emerging Technologies. 1997. *Building a Foundation for Tomorrow: Skills Standards for Information Technology.* Bellevue, Wash.: Northwest Center for Emerging Technologies.

Redburn, Tom. 1994. An economic evolution from making to thinking. *New York Times*, 18 February.

U.S. Department of Labor. 1991. SCANS (Secretary's Commission on Achieving Necessary Skills) Report for America 2000. Washington, D. C.: U. S. Department of Labor.

Wake Technical Community College
Raleigh, North Carolina

Integrated Mathematics and Physics
for Technical Programs

▶ FOCUS
- ▶ Integrating physics and mathematics courses
- ▶ Incorporating advanced technologies as teaching and learning tools

College Environment

Wake Technical Community College (Wake Tech) serves the Wake County area, which includes the capital city of Raleigh. The college adopted its present name in 1987, having been chartered as the Wake Industrial Education Center in 1958. It is accredited by the Southern Association of Colleges and Schools and has the third-largest enrollment of the 59 members of the North Carolina Community College System. It maintains three campuses and facilities, enrolling approximately 45,000 students annually in credit and non-credit courses; its full-time equivalency is 6,000. Engineering technology is one of five academic divisions. Most of its 13 departments require degree students to take 13 semester hours of mathematics and physics offered by the mathematics and physics department.

The student body is 55 percent female and 32 percent minority. Enrollment has grown by 13 percent over the past two years. The college's service area comprises a large urban population as well as a significant rural component. The area is growing rapidly, from a 1990 population in Wake County of about 410,000 to a projected 800,000 in 2020.

The college provides employees for a diverse range of businesses. Industry giants such as IBM,

Wake Technical Community College
9101 Fayetteville Road
Raleigh, NC 27603-5696
Ph: 919/662-3400
www.wake.tec.nc.us
President: Bruce I. Howell

Contact
Robert Kimball, Chair
Mathematics and Physics Department
Ph: 919/662-3602
Fax: 919/779-3660
E-mail: rkimball@gwmail.wake.tec.nc.us

Program Web Address
www.wake.tec.nc.us/math/Chimp

Glaxo Wellcome, Northern Telecom, and SAS call the Research Triangle Park (RTP) area home. RTP has attracted high-tech industry and helped make this area one of the fastest growing in the country. Most graduates in engineering technology will find work in a highly technical workplace and the expectations of these graduates are high. The college maintains a close relationship with business through industrial advisory committees. Each program uses its own advisory committee to help maintain an exemplary and relevant program, able to adapt to meet the expressed needs of industry. In addition to these formal roles, the college maintains contact with graduates, counting on them to support the college through its foundation. The foundation is helping to increase the community's awareness of the importance of the college to local business by using industrial representatives who can tell the college's story to school and community groups.

Program Profile

The ATE program at Wake Tech began in 1997 with the Committee to Help Integrate Math and Physics (CHIMP). Acknowledging the need to connect mathematics and physics, the CHIMP team writes and evaluates hands-on, multi-faceted activities for faculty to use in developing learner-centered classroom presentations. The activities engage students more thoroughly in the learning process, making the material more interesting. The activities use mathematics to support physics and physics to support mathematics. Technology is used routinely to increase understanding through simulations and modeling and as a tool for problem solving. Because the program materials are used in existing classes, no additional recruitment of students was necessary.

Kathy Hill (Athens Drive High School) and William Smith (Beaufort County Community College) collect data using the CBR during a summer workshop for community college and high school mathematics and physics faculty.

Even though what we were doing had to do with physics, we had to use mathematics to get the solution. You learn it better that way.

—Student

The physics and mathematics communities are calling for classroom teaching to reflect current knowledge about how students learn best as well as to incorporate available technology as teaching and learning tools. Program staff designed a student-centered learning approach using a sustained integrated, hands-on, problem-centered scheme for instruction in mathematics and physics. Students are expected to take responsibility for learning, using the instructor as one of the resources. They use advanced technological tools, including calculator-based and microcomputer-based laboratories, to collect data. Spreadsheets and graphing calculators are used to organize and analyze the data. Collaborating local high schools and school faculties apply the resource materials and approaches to their own work.

The program supports several integrated mathematics and physics activities aimed at strengthening student skills in applying mathematical concepts and better preparing students for a highly technical workplace. Classroom activities use physics concepts to motivate the study of mathematical concepts. Mathematics is applied to revisit physics concepts and serves to uncover the physics. Topics from algebra, trigonometry, and physics are incorporated into hands-on, collaborative activities that use technology routinely. These applied learning approaches are being field-tested in math and physics classes at the college, at local high schools, and at other two-year colleges in North Carolina and elsewhere.

Students develop skills necessary for collaborative work, including the ability to use each team member's resources, express themselves clearly, and be sensitive to individual needs while still completing a final product. At the same time, students develop skills needed for independent study, such as the ability to read critically, establish a process and a plan of action, and find resources as needed. Students expand their communication skills through the extensive use of the "elicit-confront-resolve-assess" model, a design that primes student interest, presents a problem, initiates resolution of the prob-

I learned that measurements always have errors. We need to be able to control the amount of error in an experiment and explain why errors occur.

—Student

---

lem, and requires assessment of both the process and the conclusion of the activity.

The activities demonstrate that an integrated approach to mathematics and physics helps give students a better understanding of the physics and the ability to apply the mathematics. Through publications and meetings of physics and mathematics professional organizations, the college is sharing the activities with others at the state and national levels.

Why This Approach?

Wake Tech's ATE program is based on a series of investigations of the current and future skill needs of engineering technologists. The CHIMP team tapped the knowledge and thinking of employers, professional engineers, and faculty. It also examined the published works of relevant national groups, including reports from the National Skill Standards Board, the National Research Council, the Accreditation Board of Engineering and Technology, the American Association of Physics Teachers, and the American Mathematical Association of Two-Year Colleges. The program focused on three significant needs that emerged from these investigations:

Students need to do mathematics and physics. Students engaged in meaningful, hands-on activities are more likely to enjoy their studies, be more motivated in their work, and learn more.

Students need to use mathematics and physics to solve problems. By addressing problems that require the use of mathematics or physics, students will make the connection more easily between science and their fields of study.

Students need to see technology (particularly graphing calculators and computer-based spreadsheets) as a tool that can aid their investigations and analyses. Students need to see technology as

PARTNERS

College advisory teams. Helped meet ATE goals.

High school physics and math teacher team. Reviewed new materials and served as team leaders at summer workshops.

Higher education team. Reviewed the progress of developed materials and served as summer workshop facilitators. Some facilitators were affiliated with Rowan-Cabarrus Community College, Sandhills Community College, and North Carolina State University.

Other North Carolina institutions. Field-tested materials at Isothermal Community College, Athens Drive High School, and Leesville High School.

another aid in investigation and problem solving. They need to learn to use the appropriate technology at the appropriate time.

Faculty and administrators believe that this new approach, which provides a solid base of knowledge in science, technology, mathematics, and communications skills, will produce graduates capable of succeeding in an ever-changing workplace. They think the approach will help students to make the connection between mathematics and the real world by providing a content-delivery system with hands-on activities in which mathematics and physics are integrated and taught by a multi-disciplinary (mathematics and physics) team. Faculty and administrators also feel that this approach will produce a learning environment with no distinction between class and laboratory activities, fostering effective learning through a variety of methods, including a routine use of technology and oral and written presentations.

Influences on Program Development

Several written works helped the college team develop the program by providing goals, standards, and recommendations for learning activities. They include:

MAJOR ACHIEVEMENTS

Structured integrated activities. CHIMP structured integrated activities within units that incorporate topics from Algebra and Trigonometry I and II and from Physics-Mechanics.

Faculty training. The team presented and tested the new activities in two summer 1998 workshops for faculty teams from high schools and community colleges across North Carolina. In a train-the-trainer approach, the first two-day workshop trained faculty who presented the second two-day workshop for 18 paired teams. Five of the teams were composed of faculty from community colleges; the other teams represented high schools.

Tested curriculum. The materials were tested at the college in mathematics and physics courses, at other colleges, and in high school math classes.

Dissemination. Staff actively disseminated information about the program, including making presentations to local, state, and national audiences of legislators, high school teachers, college faculty, and local residents.

- *Crossroads in mathematics, standards for introductory college mathematics before calculus.* 1995. Memphis: American Mathematical Association of Two-Year Colleges. ISBN: 0-9643890-0-2 (Describes goals and objectives appropriate for written activities).
- Secretary's Commission on Achieving Necessary Skills (SCANS). *What work requires of schools: A SCANS report for America 2000.* 1991. Washington, D.C.: U.S. Department of Labor. (Identifies industry standards related to the preparation of various technicians).
- *Critical issues in two-year college physics and astronomy.* 1991. College Park, Md.: American Association of Physics Teachers. (Recommendations aimed at creating learning activities to encourage students of all backgrounds to continue study in science and mathematics).

It's good to have experiments in which the participants develop their own process and thus use different methods to arrive at conclusions. They are then forced to justify differences in outcomes between groups.
—*Teacher and workshop participant*

Unexpected Outcomes

Mathematics and physics courses that were not part of the original project have adopted elements of it, resulting in enhanced classroom teaching and learning environments. Student feedback indicates that faculty are more responsive to students, encourage more discussion, take more questions, and are less likely to consume classroom time with long lectures. The project team is working on a model that will incorporate other content beyond mathematics and physics, including focuses on applications in business, electronics, and other technical curricula at the college.

Interestingly, the new approach is a challenge for a number of students. Some resist and dislike efforts to make them more actively engaged in the learning process. They have been trained to expect teachers to provide them with everything they need to know. When the teacher becomes a facilitator for such students, there can be friction. It also appears that if a student's earlier learning relied on memorization rather than understanding, the student may dislike problems in which there may be several possible methods or ones that aren't exactly like examples done in class. Faculty must help students adjust to an environment in which they are more responsible for their learning.

The program has improved relationships between college faculty and the teaching staff in the Wake County Public School system. Through their participation in this project and the periodic meetings between college faculty and high school staffs, the schoolteachers better understand and appreciate the level of mathematics and physics instruction at the college. They also benefit from the materials generated by the project. The ATE program at the college complemented earlier school relationships that had been developed through the local Tech Prep.

[Students] are pleased to put the mathematics to use in a meaningful activity and believe they learned the material better by doing so. The evaluations ... indicate a positive change in the students' attitudes toward mathematics.

—Faculty member

Recognition

Partly through this effort and other work supported by the National Science Foundation, the college has enhanced its reputation as a community college leader in curriculum reform and discipline integration. Press reports, in publication such as the newsletter of the North Carolina Mathematics Association of Two-Year Colleges and the local newspaper, the *News and Observer,* have helped publicize the college's work. Project staff have been invited to local, state, regional, and national meetings to discuss the work. Summer and conference workshop participants and attendees at meetings in North Carolina have been enormously positive.

College Commitment

Historically, the college administration has actively encouraged staff to pursue resources designed to stimulate instructional innovation and curriculum reform in all disciplines. The college supported the mathematics and physics departments' request to teach all mathematics courses with a laboratory component. Members of the department are working closely with another activity funded by the National Science Foundation called a capstone project. In it, English and science faculty collaborate with their peers in the mathematics and physics departments to guide associate of applied science degree students through their curriculum, which culminates in a final senior project. The capstone activity is shaped to demonstrate student proficiency in mathematics, communication, and use of technology necessary to solve an applied problem in a chosen field. Mathematics and physics faculty have visited industry locations to identify real-world mathematics applications that can be translated into

classroom curriculum. In addition, the college's already-established Tech Prep relationship with Wake County Public Schools has created many opportunities for testing and refining the new materials.

Materials Produced by the Program

Integrated activities for use in associate in applied science degree programs are available through the Wake Tech Department of Mathematics and Physics Web site, grouped in the following units:

- *Unit I: Measurement and Geometry.* Includes Facts of a Sphere, 3-D Solids, and Liquid Fill Simulation.
- *Unit II: Linear Functions.* Includes Free-Fall, 3-D Solids Revisited, Gas Laws, and Temperature Scales.
- *Unit III: Quadratic Functions.* Includes Free-Fall Revisited, Numerical vs. Graphical (Spreadsheet), Simulating a Projectile (Spreadsheet), and CBR—Motion.
- *Unit IV: Vectors and Trigonometry.* Includes Timber, Force Table, and 3-D Mapping.

Formal papers prepared by CHIMP for various presentations include:

- "Spreadsheets and the Internet: Hands-on Projects with Workplace Technology"
- "Integrated Mathematics and Physics for Technical Programs"
- "Evaluating CHIMP Activities"

Ted Maynard (Wake Technical Community College), Julia Kolb (Leesville High School), and Theresa Gauthier and Wilbur McBride (Cleveland County Community College) discuss the procedure they will use to collect data to model a physical phenomenon.

What's Next?

CHIMP plans to continue revising written material and testing it in classrooms. Information about progress will be disseminated at state and national conferences sponsored by the American Association of Physics Teachers, the American Mathematical Association of Two-Year Colleges, and the North Carolina Mathematics Association of Two-Year Colleges, as well as in Tech Prep activities. The program's long-term goal is to develop activities that completely cover the material in the college's introductory algebra/trigonometry and physics courses.

Jones County Junior College
Ellisville, Mississippi

The Southeast Consortium for Advanced Network Technology Education

▶ FOCUS

▶ Statewide infrastructure to educate and train two-year college and secondary school technology teachers in network technology

▶ Curriculum in computer network management

▶ Use of computer networks as an instructional tool in high schools and colleges

College Environment

Jones County Junior College (JCJC) is a 360-acre, single-campus institution serving eight counties in the southeastern sector of Mississippi. It is the largest of the 15 public, two-year college campuses in the state. Established in 1926, the college currently enrolls approximately 4,800 credit students. Although legislatively mandated to serve eight Mississippi counties, JCJC draws students from 46 Mississippi counties and eight states. The average JCJC faculty salary is $42,000—well above the average faculty salary for the southeastern United States. Twenty-three percent of the students are African American and 2 percent are Asian, Hispanic, and Native American. The average age is 23 years, younger than the national community college average of 29. Of the two-year colleges in Mississippi, JCJC has the largest percentage of graduates or completers seeking baccalaureate degrees. Seventy-one percent of the students are in academic transfer programs, 23 percent are in two-year technical education programs, and 6 percent are in one-year vocational certificate programs. The JCJC student body is 55 percent female.

The college's technical programs draw more women, more minorities, and more older students

Jones County Junior College
900 South Court Street
Ellisville, MS 39437
Ph: 601/477-4100
www.jcjc.cc.ms.us
President: Ronald Whitehead

Contacts
Catherine Perry Cotten
Director of Information and Research
Ph: 601/477-4115
Fax: 601/477-4166
E-mail: catherine.cotten@jcjc.cc.ms.us

Robert Landrum
Program Director
Computer Information Systems Technology
Ph: 601-477-4080
Fax: 601-477-4220
E-mail: robert.landrum@jcjc.cc.ms.us

Program Web Address
www.partnership.jcjc.cc.ms.us

than other programs do. Students in the technical programs are 62 percent female and 25 percent minority (Native American, African American, Asian, and Hispanic), with an average age of 25. By nature of the funding, all technical and vocational students are enrolled as full-time students. Each program has well-defined student competencies in all areas related to the program. This includes academic as well as workplace skills.

JCJC requires all students to be computer literate and assigns all students e-mail addresses upon enrollment. The college has one computer available for every three students. Nearly all (99 percent) of the college's courses require the computer to be used as a tool for completion of course requirements.

Every campus building, classroom, and office has direct access to the Internet. The library facilities have online access to collections through the college Web site. In addition, the administration, faculty, and students have access to Magnolia, the state digital library funded by the Mississippi legislature for use by every library and education institution in the state. Students and faculty may access Magnolia and the JCJC library holdings from home, dorm, or business.

The two-year technical programs in computer technology and many other technical programs have strong articulation agreements with the University of Southern Mississippi School of Engineering Technology. All of the occupational education programs have advisory committees composed of business, industry, and education partners. At least every two years, curricula in these programs are subject to revision under the guidance of these advisory committees. Due to marketplace demands, the Computer Information

Jones provides the education you need to enter the job market.
—*Former student, Dominic Tynes, Cothern Computer Group, Jackson, Mississippi*

Systems Technology (CIST) curriculum has been revised every year since the inclusion of the network technology curriculum.

The average job placement rate for all occupational education programs is 95 percent. Successful placement of the completers and graduates is a requirement for continued funding of the programs.

Jones County Junior College has been the pilot site for all two-year college curricula in the areas of local area network technology, wide area network technology, and Internet design courses. Once the college completes the pilot phase of these programs, the new curriculum goes through a rewrite before the remainder of the state's 14 public two-year colleges may adopt the two-year technical degree programs.

At least 18 hours of the technical program's requirements for graduation are in core courses. In addition, most students in CIST have two areas of emphasis—selected from programming, local area network support, and wide area network support. Internet applications and programming are elective courses.

Jones County Junior College relegates workforce training to its One-Stop Career Center. Mississippi's Workforce Education Act of 1994 established Skill/Tech One-Stop Centers to provide a regionally based system in Mississippi for the education and training of the state's workers. The community and junior college Skill/Tech One-Stop Centers work with a District Workforce Council in planning strategies to meet the needs of Mississippi's business and industry. JCJC combines the expertise of the career center and the technical programs to offer information technology credit courses and non-credit customized training for business and industry. Offerings include training in professional office software, programming, network

JCJC has confidence in and hires its own graduates. In the picture is a former student who now runs the network for the JCJC Computer Aided Learning Lab which includes 175 network computers with over 1,000 software programs.

support, Web master skills, and fiber optic cabling. The needs of the business workforce determine the frequency of these offerings.

The college grants associate in arts and associate in applied science degrees, as well as vocational certificates. It offers a comprehensive set of educational opportunities through academic, vocational-technical, and personal enrichment programs that meet local needs.

The college's computer technology programs are two of the largest technical programs of their kind in the state. The Computer Information Systems Technology program was the first to implement the networking option initiated and designed by the Mississippi State Department of Education Vocational-Technical Division and the Mississippi community and junior college system. The programs are formally articulated with the University of Southern Mississippi. The Mississippi State Personnel Board has designated the college's CIST program as the model education program for computer network technicians hired by the state. Any graduate of a two-year college seeking employment within state agencies must have the same education and same level of technical skills as a graduate of the JCJC Computer Information Systems Technology program.

The population of Mississippi—approximately 2.7 million within 47,233 square miles of land—is 36 percent African American, 63 percent white, and the remainder Hispanic, Asian, and Native American. Nearly two-thirds live in the southern half of the state. Mississippi's growth rate from 1995 to 2025 is expected to be 17 percent. According to the U.S. Bureau of Labor Statistics, Mississippi's rate of job growth is predicted to be 8 percent, compared to 5 percent nationally. In addition, the total college enrollment growth is above the national percentage of 15 percent. The college-going rate is also increasing: Mississippi's total college enrollment growth is 16 percent (National Center for Education Statistics), and 25 percent of that growth is in the two-year colleges. Two-year colleges in Mississippi now enroll 43 percent of all postsecondary students. When enrollment growth, tuition increases, and inflation are factored in, per-student funding in Mississippi increased 13 percent, compared to 6 percent for the nation.

The Mississippi Gulf Coast is one of the fastest growing areas in the United States.

This program and Jones were a springboard to a fantastic career. Today I am the owner and CEO of an Internet development company.
—John Trimble,
NETCRAFTERS, Cincinnati

Mississippi is the home of Morgan Freeman and Leontyne Price, as well as writers William Faulkner, William Raspberry, and Eudora Welty. It is also home to MCI/WorldCom, SkyTel, NATCOM, Trilogy Communications, and Peavy Electronics. Many other information technology and telecommunication industries have regional offices in Mississippi, and the state is also home to the supercomputer facilities of the Naval Oceanographic Command Headquarters and the Army Corps of Engineers.

Wood-related products make a huge contribution to Mississippi's economy, in the manufacture of furniture and the making of other wood products. Gaming is a growing industry in the state, and Mississippi is second only to Nevada in that area.

Program Profile

Jones Country is creating a trained cadre of middle and high school teachers and community college faculty in electronic network technology. It is a statewide program. The project also involves the development of a computer network management curriculum for two-year college students and a related one for high school students. The dual curriculum component of the project will enhance existing Tech Prep programs and will lay the foundation for a smooth transition from high school to community college in information technology. This will also enhance the transition of the information technology (IT) students to baccalaureate programs.

Teacher preparation is a significant element of the program, since many of the participants in the IT curriculum are teachers in grades 7 through 12. The program trains them to introduce and maintain IT in the schools and to teach a related networking curriculum. Specifically, the program aims to:

- establish both a training program to instruct secondary/postsecondary teachers and a two-year degree curriculum for students in local area network technology, wide area

PARTNERS

In addition to the central collaboration among Jones County Junior College, four regionally dispersed community colleges in the state, and the University of Mississippi, the program involves partnerships with several other organizations and institutions.

Community college coalition. Copiah-Lincoln Community College, Itawamba Community College, Mississippi Delta Community College, and Mississippi Gulf Coast Community College. Recruited teachers for IT training workshops who later trained other college and high school instructors throughout the state.

University of Southern Mississippi School of Engineering Technology. Refined and improved JCJC-university articulation agreements, redesigned curriculum, and improved student advisement. A strong supporter of the two-year college transfer student, the university developed the four-year curriculum to go with the JCJC pilot LAN and WAN curriculum. It also offers a master's degree that complements the local area network (LAN) and wide area network (WAN) programs.

Mississippi State Department of Education. Facilitated the involvement of all public middle and high school teachers in the education and training program established by JCJC.

Standing advisory curriculum committees. Advise IT program through active involvement of representatives of employers, government agencies, and education organizations. The statewide curriculum rewrite committees for the two-year public college system also involve business and industry representatives.

Cisco Systems, Inc. Worked with the college to develop a Wide Area Network and to develop an "Internetworking" technology curriculum, of which the Cisco Networking Academy program is a part.

Unfortunately, many of the students graduating from colleges and universities today are not prepared for the challenges they face in the market. JCJC has consistently proven that they have the ability and desire to provide the educational environment and structure which allows their graduates to quickly become productive in the workplace.
—Don Landrum, SIRIUS Computer Solutions, San Antonio

network technology, computer servicing technology, and telecommunications technology (the student degree program and the teacher workshops prepare the participants for certification in Novell, Windows 2000), Cisco, A+, and Internet webmaster)
- educate a core of two-year college faculty who will be qualified to implement statewide the approved networking curriculum for technical students and to use computer networks as instructional tools
- educate a core of middle and secondary school faculty who will be qualified to teach the complementary networking curriculum and to manage and use computer networks for instruction
- provide training and resources for using the World Wide Web as a teaching and learning resource

The college began with a coalition of four geographically dispersed community colleges in the state (Copiah-Lincoln Community College in Wesson, Itawamba Community College in Fulton, Mississippi Delta Community College in Moorhead, and Mississippi Gulf Coast Community College in Perkinston). The University of Mississippi helped develop Web sites for the program. The University of Southern Mississippi School of Engineering Technology developed the four-year articulated curriculum for network support, which complements rather than duplicates the two-year college curriculum.

These students have proven to be professional, qualified, and valuable assets to the company.
—*Glen Hanson, MCI/WorldCom, Clinton, Mississippi*

Through an innovative instructional model for workshops, the secondary and postsecondary teachers work in learning teams. The teams participate in a classroom setting that fully integrates lecture and laboratory activities. The teachers work with hardware, software, and the wiring necessary for a functional local area network.

The program fits nicely with the Mississippi Master Plan for Educational Technology, which outlines a process for expanding investment in advanced technology as learning and instructional tools in K-12 schools. Jones County Junior College's Advanced Technological Education project addresses what is called Phase 3 of the state's master plan. Phase 3 addresses the knowledge and skills needed to understand, implement, modify, and use LAN systems.

Why This Approach?

The JCJC program responds to a number of identified national, state, and local needs. For example, the U.S. Department of Commerce reports that between 1996 and 2006, the United States will need over 1.3 million new skilled IT workers to fill newly created jobs and to replace workers leaving the field. Within Mississippi, predictions call for a 54 percent increase in the need for IT workers. In the midst of these conditions, the communications technology is changing daily. Network developments have greatly influenced business. The U.S. Department of Commerce had predicted that by 2000, 20 percent of all business commerce would occur on the World Wide Web. Internet traffic growth is now approximately 200 percent each year. Voice, data, and video systems are moving toward convergence. Soon it will not be unusual for one unit to handle all three systems. In the future, people will interact with computers using the human voice more often than they will use the keyboard or mouse. As these systems converge, automation will increase and job requirements will change. According to the

president and CEO of Ayrix Technologies, 60 percent of the jobs available in 2000 will require skills possessed by only 20 percent of the current workforce. The implications for education, training, and other professional development activities are crystal clear.

Employers visit the college in the fall and early spring to interview and hire students who will graduate in May. In addition, the Computer Information System Technology students have the opportunity to participate in the JCJC work-based learning program. Assisted by the work-based learning coordinator, the students get paid and also gain job experience in their chosen computer technology area or areas. Jones County Junior College graduates have been hired in more than 25 counties in Mississippi and in 13 states.

Mississippi is the home of some international leaders in the communications industry. They are significant employers of the college's IT graduates as well as important resources for guiding the college's curriculum. Each of these companies projects significant business expansion and a need for additional skilled IT workers.

The state personnel board, the agency that controls public sector hiring, recognized the need for advanced training for information workers. In a letter to JCJC president Ronald Whitehead in 1998, the board's director, J. K. Stringer, Jr., summarized the state situation: "Like many public organizations, we found ourselves in the

In all likelihood, these employees will be from the local community and will have received much, if not all, of their information technology education and training from their local junior/community colleges. In order for Novell to have a strong presence in the workplace, we need strong partners like JCJC to educate and train individuals on our software products. Novell is very pleased with the quality of computer professionals JCJC has produced.
—*Drew Dennis, Novell, Dallas*

MAJOR ACHIEVEMENTS

Train-the-trainer workshop. Conducted an initial four-week faculty workshop for college and high school instructors to become certified network administrators.

Regional workshops. Managed the presentation of regional training workshops conducted by faculty and teacher teams—graduates of the train-the-trainer workshop—at the five collaborating community colleges. Designed and applied a summer workshop training model that was used in subsequent summer workshops. Provided workshops in Windows NT administration/management (summer 1999).

Curriculum. Developed curriculum and offered computer technology classes for high school and community college (first classes held spring 1998).

Certification. Prepared for A+ certification in PC maintenance (spring 1998).

Web site. Developed the program Web site. Beginning in 1999, offered Web master certification education and skills workshops.

Conferences. Conducted two national conferences in June 1998 on project issues, drawing previous workshop participants as well as college leaders, state agency officials, legislators, business people, high school and college faculty, and representatives from state and national foundations. Hosted a three-day National Science Foundation national conference in February 1999, which focused on information technology programs in community colleges. Hosted the Gulf States IT Workforce Conference (June 1998), a regional U.S. Department of Commerce town hall meeting on technology, one of four meetings the department sponsored across the country. Hosted and organized national conferences on information technology (1998 and 2000), with support from the Hardin Foundation and Computer Prep, an IT company.

mid-1990s with an information technology workforce that was erroneously classified and underpaid. We also found that the knowledge, skills, and abilities required of our information technology employees, to include new employees, had changed radically in a very short period of time... We expect the information technology needs of state government to continue to increase along with a corresponding need for more qualified employees throughout the state. In all likelihood, these employees will be from the local community and will have received much, if not all, of their information technology education and training from their local junior/community colleges."

Influences on Program Development

The rapid changes occurring in the technology world spurred Jones County Junior College to develop education and training programs that would meet business needs. Working with the American Technical Educators Association, the Association of Information Technology Professionals, the National Business Association, the National Association of Vocational Education, and the Cisco Networking Academies, JCJC instructors developed program and workshop course materials for networking administration. They purchased books and other lab materials and developed an extensive set of workshop guidelines. Because the technology content changes so quickly, it has been necessary to constantly revise materials to keep them current and dynamic. JCJC staff visited other community colleges with ATE programs to compare notes on curriculum development for similar network administration programs.

Faculty Recruitment

A committee composed of representatives of the college coalition determined which faculty would participate in the initial four-week training program. It used the following criteria to make selections:

- potential of the applicant to absorb the knowledge and acquire the skills necessary to improve teaching performance, and a recommendation from a supervisor.
- need for the knowledge and skills in current and future teaching assignments.

JCJC has worked very closely with Cisco in developing a two-year WAN internetworking technology curriculum of which the Cisco Networking Academies program is a part. Students successfully completing the curriculum will be able to demonstrate the ability to implement and maintain internetworking projects.

—Mark Rittinier, Cisco Systems, Jackson, Mississippi

- prior successful participation in professional development activities.
- commitment to attend the entire four-week workshop.

The initial faculty workshops were competitive—only one of every two applicants was accepted. Some sites had more applicants than others. The participants rated the workshops highly. Because the teachers had a current need for the workshop materials, they appreciated the opportunity to learn the content.

The initial workshop took place in summer 1997 and was designed to train trainers responsible for duplicating the training in their own region of the state. Thirty teachers and faculty participated in the workshop—15 middle/high school instructors and 15 community college faculty. Participants were paid a stipend to attend but received full payment only after passing the examination to become a certified Novell administrator (CNA). For some, the certification requirement was a frightening goal—but a satisfying one when they earned their IT certifications after the training.

Faculty stay in contact with each other after the workshops and receive technical assistance through the program Web site and statewide meetings that were already built into the vocational-technical infrastructure in Mississippi. In accordance

with the college's hopes for the program, some workshop participants are now giving teacher workshops of their own.

The workshops continued in succeeding summers but expanded to five two-year college sites in each region of the state. Workshops held in the summer of 2000 targeted Cisco Networking Academy instructors and certified Internet Webmasters, offering Web Design for Beginners. To date, nearly 80 percent of all workshop participants (middle and high school teachers and community college faculty) have passed the CNA certification exam.

Jones County Junior College established a training facility on its campus for year-round IT training for educators and other members of the workforce from business and industry. This is a good example of how the college assimilated work from the NSF grants into its other programs. In addition, the college initiated IT Online! This is a pilot program developed with a business partner to deliver IT training and education via distance learning. IT Online! has on-campus laboratories and testing and includes all of the technical information and certifications currently offered by JCJC and the Southeast Consortium for Advanced Network Technology Education. After initial non-credit offerings in the fall of 2000, the college will offer the courses for credit in 2001.

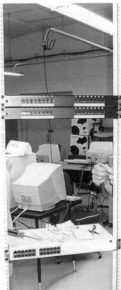

Two-year college instructors completing the laboratory activities for the Cisco Networking Academy Training on the JCJC campus. Both instructors have been trained in LAN systems and have implemented the LAN curriculum developed by JCJC.

When we began developing the desired curriculum for information technology graduates, we found that JCJC had taken the lead and had already developed such a program. That program has now been certified by the state's director of information technology services.

—J. K. Stringer, Jr., Mississippi State Personnel Board

Unexpected Outcomes

Jones County Junior College saw significant growth in its CIST program as well as in all of its IT programs. IT enrollment more than doubled between spring 1997 and fall 1999, from 105 to 240 students. The college hired five additional faculty and established a secondary networking curriculum in local area networks and wide area networks (LAN and WAN). Possibly due to the tremendous state and national publicity generated by the ATE program, the college attracted large numbers of students returning to school to acquire skills in the advanced network technologies. These new junior college students already have bachelor's, master's, and doctoral degrees.

The excitement and accomplishments of the ATE grant generated important attitude changes at the college, which is justly proud of the program. Administrators, faculty, and staff now promote IT wherever they go.

Altogether, the JCJC consortium has had a large impact. It trained faculty from 54 of Mississippi's 82 counties. Through training and mentoring, it affected faculty in 11 additional states, including a tribal college. The training also affected 108 public schools and more than 51,000 students through trained faculty (209 middle and high school teachers). Trained faculty (82 in 25 two-year colleges) have reached approximately 25,000 two-year college students. The training reached twice as many women as men.

Recognition

Jones County Junior College has become quite visible as a result of its ATE program. Cisco Systems selected the college to be the Cisco Networking Academy Regional Academy for the postsecondary institutions in Mississippi. Staff presented at various national conferences, including the 35th National Conference on Technical Education (March 1998). During the first two years of the program, they presented at more than 20 different local, state, regional, and national professional meetings.

Individual recognition has come as well. Phi Theta Kappa, through its Improving Science & Technology Education at Community Colleges project, selected the JCJC principal investigator as one of its mentors to assist three additional colleges in their efforts to establish or improve information technology curricula. Two of the project instructors have been chosen by the American Technical Educators Association as National Technical Educator of the Year, the most recent in 1999.

Numerous publications highlighted the JCJC program goals and achievements. In addition to local and regional newspapers, articles have appeared in the following: *ATEA Journal* (December-January, 1997-98); *Pacesetter,* from the U.S. Office of Technology Policy (1998); *1,001 Exemplary Practices in America's Two-Year Colleges,* edited by Rouche, Parnell, and Kuttler, in McGraw-Hill's College Custom Series; Phi Theta Kappa's "Improving Science & Technology News;" and the *Community College Times* and *Community College Journal* of the American Association of Community Colleges. The U.S. Department of Commerce's Office of Technology Policy noted Jones County's work in *The Digital Work Force: Building Infotech Skills at the Speed of Innovation.*

The JCJC program is prominent within the state and is listed on the Web site of the Mississippi State Department of Education Vocational-Technical Office. The college also has exhibited at the Mississippi Academy of Sciences annual meeting.

College Commitment

Jones County Junior College has institutionalized the academic programs and the teacher workshop developed with the ATE grant. The college is firmly committed to sustaining facilities and staffing to support the IT program, which expanded exponentially as a result of the new network support technology program. It will offer the teacher workshops through the JCJC One-Stop Career Center. Although participants will be expected to pay a workshop fee, school systems are still interested. Business and industry workforce members will also participate in these workshops.

Due to the success of Jones County Junior College in its ATE project and other advanced technology endeavors, the State of Mississippi legislatively appropriated $4,000,000 for an advanced technology facility on the JCJC campus. The college is responsible for matching monies and is well on the way to doing so. The president of the college initiated these activities and is working with the JCJC Foundation to raise the monies. The JCJC Advanced Technology Center will be built within the Jones County Technology Park.

Leveraged Funds

The college has benefited from local and state support. External groups have provided approximately $250,000 for equipment and other needs. For example, the Mississippi State Department of Education Vocation-Technical Division matched project equipment funds with $154,168. COHO Industries of Laurel donated $15,000 to the college foundation for the Computer Information Systems Technology Department. Custom Micro gave $9,000 to support project activities. The Mississippi-based Hardin Foundation provided a total of

$36,398, including funds to support a national conference.

What's Next?

The college continues to expand the work begun with the ATE grant. The program Web site is under constant refinement, and new workshops on special networking concepts are in development. Post-grant plans include developing certificate or degree programs in computer servicing technology and telecommunications technology. Partnering with the One-Stop Career Center, the college is developing a Web Master Certification Training Center for educators, businesses, and students.

Materials Produced by the Program

The college developed significant curriculum materials as a result of its ATE grant. An extensive curriculum package for the LAN and the WAN programs includes academic and workplace skills as well as necessary instructor competencies and equipment specifications for the laboratories. Materials for the four-week training workshops include detailed and day-to-day outlines and lecture and laboratory activities. An important component is the wiring design of the laboratories for the teaching of the LAN curriculum. In addition, an eight-page brochure called *Technology Partnership for Computer Networking Training* describes the overall program at Jones County Junior College.

Oklahoma State University-Okmulgee
Okmulgee, Oklahoma

Preparing High-Performance Technicians in Distinctive Manufacturing Technology (DMT): An Innovative Approach

▶ **FOCUS**
▶ Manufacturing technology
▶ Student-centered learning

College Environment

Among the oil wells, Native American tribes, and hills of eastern Oklahoma lies an anomaly in education. Students in the Distinctive Manufacturing Technology (DMT) program at Oklahoma State University's technology campus in Okmulgee are setting new standards for retention, motivation, internship salaries, and more. Faculty in this Advanced Technological Education program voluntarily work more than the required workload to make it succeed, and DMT administrators are just as excited about this new approach to learning.

The historical national capital city for the Muscogee (Creek) Tribe, one of 39 Native American tribes in Oklahoma, Okmulgee is a community of 17,000 people located about 35 miles south of Tulsa in a rural, east-central location. The OSU-Okmulgee campus opened in 1946 to enroll 500 war veterans for instruction in agricultural and mechanical trades. Its mission is statewide and sharply focused: "To serve as the lead institution of higher education in Oklahoma and the region for comprehensive, high quality, advancing-technology programs and services to prepare and sustain a diverse student body as competitive members of a world-class work force and contributing members of society." It still serves as the technical college for the state.

Oklahoma State University-Okmulgee
1801 East 4th Street
Okmulgee, OK 74447
Ph: 918/293-4678
www.osu-okmulgee.edu
Provost: Robert E. Klabenes

Contact
Rick Allison, Principal Investigator
Department of Manufacturing
Ph: 918/293-5124
Fax: 918/293-4633
E-mail: ralison@osu-okmulgee.edu

Program Web Address
www.osu-okmulgee.edu/dmt/index.htm

OSU-Okmulgee offers the associate in applied science degree and has 40 advanced technological programs that average 90 semester credit hours, equivalent to a three-year degree. The college's fall 1998 enrollment was 2,266, two-thirds male and largely (80 percent) first-time college students. Like most other community colleges, the average age is 26. The college's racial mix is 15.5 percent Native American, 7 percent African American, 75 percent white, and 2.5 percent other students. Although the college offers on-campus housing for 700 students, 70 percent live off campus. One in five students has not graduated from high school and 48 percent have needed remediation in one or more general education subjects. Approximately 70 percent of the students have received some form of financial aid. Nearly all of the 135 faculty are full-time, year-round employees, and the student to faculty ratio is 10.3 to 1. The college employs about 20 adjunct faculty each semester, mostly to offer instruction in customized technological courses for business and industry.

Program Profile

The central purpose of the ATE program was to develop and pilot test an environment that promotes deep learning through learner-centered activities. Achieving this purpose required altering the traditional educational structure in the college's existing manufacturing technology program from teacher-centered to learner-centered. To acknowledge this new approach, the new program was called Distinctive Manufacturing Technology.

DMT prepares world-class manufacturing technologists. In distinctive manufacturing firms, designers, engineers, and production workers collaborate in seamless teams to ensure that products and services meet consumer requirements, that new technologies are applied quickly, and that operations run at optimum efficiency to maximize return on investment. The key role of high-performance technologists is to act as caretaker of the production process. They create bridges among product designers, engineers, machine operators, and marketers, with customer satisfaction and bottom-line results always in mind.

DMT student Joe Petree learns manufacturing skills on a state-of-the-art surface grinder as he completes a project pursuant to the NSF funded Distinctive Manufacturing Technology program at OSU-Okmulgee.

We have a 'just-in-time' learning style rather than having an instructor lecture for weeks at a time and students having no idea how it applies to the real world. You learn things when you need to know them, not when the teacher needs to teach them.

—DMT student

The pedagogical approach for the program is called just-in-time instruction. The traditional linear, sequenced approach to learning development, characterized by heavy doses of lecture and memorization, is replaced with spontaneous learning in integrated clusters. Real-world problems and projects drive all learning, beginning with basic tasks and moving progressively through increasingly complex assignments. Traditional disciplines (communications, math, engineering, science, etc.) occur in the instruction as they are needed to solve problems and complete projects. Multidisciplinary faculty teams serve as facilitators for student learning.

Curriculum. Because curriculum is driven by both facilitator and student objectives, it has the following nontraditional characteristics:
- elasticity
- mastery-driven
- rapid pace
- often socialistic (working together)
  - competency-assessed
  - drama-driven
  - authentic/real world
  - not constrained by time

Students learn quickly that they are crucial partners in their own learning. By the end of their first week, they have teamed with other students to design, manufacture, and market a product. Teams of students work together throughout the program to solve problems or develop a product, most often verifying the quality of their work using professional tools and applying their solutions in real-world settings. The result is learning that is fun, spontaneous, rapid, deep, authentic, engaging, and mastery-driven.

I feel like I got what every college student wants but few get. You come out, and you're actually worth something as an employee.

—Graduate of the A.A.S. program

Competencies in DMT's curriculum are broad-based. Heavy emphasis is given to those skills that travel easily from job category to job category. Most of these are what DMT refers to as "soft skills," such as communicating, teamwork, problem solving, and diversity management. As for technical competencies, in DMT students do not learn a specific machine (e.g., Saturn robot, manual lathe) as much as they learn about machining (e.g., robotics, manual machining) in general. Administrators and others may be concerned about losing depth for breadth. But in DMT, the depth is on transferable competencies such as communication, teamwork, or problem solving, while the breadth is on skills that are not easily transferable and may very well be outdated in a few years anyway.

The traditional academic system of enrolled hours and semesters does not adequately reflect a competency-driven curriculum such as that of DMT. Students stay in the program until they demonstrate mastery of the required competencies. They will spend approximately six semesters, year-round, and be granted an A.A.S. degree for 90 semester hours in engineering technology.

Phases. The DMT program is composed of five general phases:

Phase 1: Orientation—gaining familiarity with the world of manufacturing and manufacturing enterprises.

Phase 2: Exploration—developing fundamental competencies in workplace effectiveness, personal productivity, technical skill sets, and supporting capabilities.

Phase 3: Specialization—developing specialized competencies in one or more selected technical skill sets, while continuing to enhance competencies in other areas.

Phase 4: Workplace Advanced—developing buffering, brokering, entrepreneurship, and other advanced high-performance technician competencies through one semester of paid internship.

Phase 5: Capstone—applying advanced high

performance technician competencies to solve a significant problem in a manufacturing enterprise in the final semester.

The phases relate to developmental levels, not to specific periods of time. Estimated time frames range from a few weeks to a few months per phase.

Phase	Estimated Time Frame
Orientation	a few weeks
Exploration	several months
Specialization	several months
Workplace Advanced	a few months
Capstone	a few months

Segments, modules, activities. Learning experiences are organized as segments and may occur in almost any sequence, unless they are prerequisites. The focus of each segment is a product, project, or problem. Segments consist of modules, which are activity groupings culminating in the final product, project, or problem of the segment. Within each module are the specific activities that drive the entire curriculum. The drama-driven characteristic of DMT means that each segment or module has a story. There is a problem to be solved, a project to be completed, and a beginning and an end.

The goal of the DMT curriculum is for students to achieve and demonstrate relevant competencies. However, while the curriculum identifies the primary competencies to be addressed and facilitators help determine competency level through their guidance, it is the students who, through their own initiative and abilities, ultimately determine the competency level obtained. Another way of saying this is that, for any given competency, the DMT curriculum allows students to realize their desired potential.

Assessments are developed at any level (segment, module, activity, etc.) of the curriculum for which they apply. The five phases of the curriculum are sequential, but segments may be assigned

What really gets me out of bed in the morning is DMT.

—DMT student

to any phase in which they are appropriate. Modules within segments are typically sequential, as are learning tasks and activities.

Field experiences. Field experiences are a major aspect of the DMT curriculum. The program goal is to have students in the field at least once every four weeks during the orientation and exploration phases, at least once a week during the specialization phase, and almost continually during the internship phase. Types of field experience are listed below:

Field Type	Description
Exploratory	tours, interviews, observation, etc.
Shadowing	one to three days with one or more employees
Mini-internship	one to three weeks, unpaid
Internship	semester-long paid experience
Capstone	students identify a problem, develop a solution, and present it to industry

Database. A comprehensive database is maintained by the project. It contains student information, curriculum, competency areas, resources for each curriculum activity—including outside resources, tracking of deliverables, assessment tools, records of assessments, and reports on the status of each student in each competency area.

The public tours the authentic manufacturing facility located in the Donald W. Reynolds Technology Center at OSU-Okmulgee during Advancing Technology Showcase Day.

A typical day may include doing a simulation on how to run a business, making a slide presentation to sell a plan for a project to manufacture, developing a CAD model, working on a CNC machine, and tracking production resources using a database.

—DMT student

Why This Approach?

Recent data from the Bureau of the Census show a trend toward increasing numbers of 18- to 24-year olds as well as an increase in the number of college degrees granted each year. Nevertheless, schools are not producing adequate numbers of technicians to fill manufacturers' needs. DMT's socialized, student-centered approach at OSU-Okmulgee builds a natural support system, creating a higher retention rate. Education literature supports in theory what DMT is finding out in application: This approach means fewer dropouts and more graduates (Greathouse 1986, Stasz et al. 1993). DMT's individualized approach is attractive to a wider variety of students, therefore opening the door to manufacturing education.

Manufacturing firms that are distinctive in their approach to performance are replacing traditional manufacturing firms (Bailey 1990, Buchanan 1990, Buck and Barrick 1987, Drucker 1986), and the nature of manufacturing work is shifting from a manual orientation to a knowledge orientation, shifting productivity emphasis from quantity to quality. This industry trend creates an explicit need for high-performance technicians who see the business of manufacturing from a holistic view. At the same time, many people still see manufacturing as a path not to be taken by bright students.

In a direct effort to eradicate this stigma, DMT has set standards for entrance at a higher level than other technical programs on the OSU-Okmulgee campus. DMT'S fast-paced, spontaneous, drama-driven, student-centered, learning-centered approach attracts quality students. Among the evidence is the increase in ACT scores for entering students (compared to the old manufacturing program).

The DMT program was developed in response to reported industry discontent with the preparedness of entry-level employees and a demand for a transformation of technical education. Although there has been much dialogue about educational reform, most American education still is time-bound, place-bound, role-bound, and bureaucracy-bound (O'Banion 1997). The DMT curriculum is project-driven and learning is integrated. Students become proficient in a wide variety of skills. They graduate with soft skills identified by employers as necessary to become outstanding performers (SCANS 1991). Students in traditional systems are being taught, but many are not learning (Dykman 1997, O'Banion 1997). The curriculum in DMT is competency-driven, multidisciplinary, and employer/industry approved. It makes learning competency-assessed, mastery-driven, and authentic for the real world.

DMT students progress not by getting 60 percent of the answers right on a paper-and-pen test, nor by putting in a required amount of "seat time" or a set number of weeks (a semester), but by demonstrating competencies, regardless of time frame. DMT's entire curriculum is built around projects and problems derived primarily from partnering companies, many of whom serve on the DMT advisory council.

Influences on Program Development

Central to the development of this unique approach was staff experience with the Summer Manufacturing Academy, a program that helped faculty and administrators to sharpen and verify the quality of student-

PARTNERS

The North East Oklahoma Manufacturers Council. Provides site visits, projects, shadowing experiences and other technical assistance to students. A 43-member consortium of small and medium-sized manufacturing companies, the council's purposes include providing leadership to promote continuously improved manufacturing operations, foster employee development, modernize technology, support industrial education, and promote corporate citizenship.

Concurrent Technologies Corporation (CTC). Developed a module and resource materials for the Life-Cycle Design curriculum; served as the project's co-principal investigator for the first phase of the project. CTC, which specializes in applied research, sponsors paid internships for fifth-semester students at its Johnstown, Pennsylvania, facility.

Regional Technology Strategies, Inc. Key project network broker. The North Carolina-based firm is dedicated to strengthening public policy and development that promote a high-wage industry economy and manages a national networking initiative (USNet).

Consortium for Manufacturing Competitiveness. Promotes the use of 15 southern technologically advanced, associate degree-granting colleges to strengthen the region's industrial base; helps these colleges determine the best industrial practices. Consortium minority groups are represented on the council through the chief of the Muskogee Creek Nation, a member of the Cherokee Nation, and African Americans through the Greenwood Chamber of Commerce in Tulsa.

Educational institutions and organizations. The following serve on DMT's advisory council: Tulsa Public School System (focusing on recruitment of Hispanic students); Green County Vo-Tech school (operating three joint programs with the college and co-sponsoring summer manufacturing academies for middle school and high school students); Oklahoma Vo-Tech system (organizes faculty training workshops); and the Society of Manufacturing Engineers (SME) (providing scholarships for the Manufacturing Technology Department).

Other corporate partners. The following provide a number of resources to the program: Ford Motor Company, General Motors Corporation, Chrysler Corporation, Caterpillar Incorporated, Ditch Witch, Texaco Incorporated, SEMATECH, Rolex USA, and others.

Green County Vocational-Technical High School. Partners with OSU-Okmulgee for dual enrollment of students in three areas: engineering graphics, manufacturing, and electronics.

MAJOR ACHIEVEMENTS

Innovative approach. The project developed and tested a transportable approach to preparing high-performance technicians that is innovative in the content of the learning program and in the nature of the learning experience. Analogous to the prototypal workplace, students work in teams, problem-solving and communicating with others. Faculty act as environment specialists, setting the scenarios, then becoming sources of wisdom and direction.

Faculty development. The innovative approach is "just-in-time," contextually based, asynchronous, and student-oriented. To implement this approach, faculty have changed from an instruction-based to a learning-based paradigm. Before this project began, faculty were delivering instruction; now they are facilitating learning. To aid in faculty conversion, staff teams created a schematic of the dimensions of teaching and learning that underlie this new approach. The dimensions were drawn from research in cognitive learning theory (Ashcraft 1994), the nature of successful technical preparation programs, and the needs expressed by the advisory council that guides the program. To gauge their progress in adopting and applying these dimensions, faculty were placed on a scale that captured assessments of their performances before the project began, at the point the scale was completed, and at the completion of the first phase of the funded effort. A random sample of non-DMT faculty was used for comparison. The comparison showed that DMT faculty achieved major positive changes in their understanding of the content and approach required by this new teaching and learning vision. Non-DMT faculty reported no significant change over the period of the grant. Furthermore, the project staff are creating a partnership between Oklahoma State University and the State Department of Vocational Education to establish an intensive program to enhance the skills of vocational educators in the state. Finally, the project is packaging the DMT approach and disseminating the concepts and procedures in national and international professional forums (see Recognition section).

continued on next page...

DMT [Distinctive Manufacturing Technology] is such a radical change from any type of education I have ever known that it is very hard to explain and convey my feelings and excitement.

—DMT *student*

focused, project-centered, learner-community learning. The college also employed a technical consultant who helped shape the general scope of the program and to sharpen specific aspects of it. Print materials were useful. Some principal ones include:

- Angelo, Thomas A., and K. Patricia Cross. 1993. *Classroom assessment techniques: a handbook for college teachers.* San Francisco, Calif.: Jossey-Bass Publishers.
- Barr R. B., and J. Tagg. 1995. From teaching to learning: A new paradigm for undergraduate education. *Change 27* (6): 13-25 (November/December).
- O'Banion, Terry. 1997. *Creating more learning-centered community colleges.* Mission Viego, Calif.: League for Innovation in the Community College.
- O'Banion, Terry. 1997. *A learning college for the 21st Century.* Phoenix, Ariz.: Oryx Press.
- Herman, J. L., P. R. Aschbacher, and L. Winters. 1992. *A practical guide to alternative assessment.* Alexandria: Association for Supervision and Curriculum Development.
- Lazear, David. 1991. *Seven ways of knowing: Teaching for multiple intelligences.* Palatine, Ill: Skylight Publishers.
- Lazear, David. 1994. *Seven pathways of learning: Teaching students and parents about multiple intelligences.* Tucson, Ariz.: Zephyr Press.
- Gardner, Howard. 1993. *Multiple intelligences: The theory in practice.* New York: Basic Books.
- Gardner, Howard. 1991. *The unschooled mind: How children think and how schools should teach.* New York: Basic Books.
- Naisbett, John. 1986. *The new American boom.* Washington, D.C.: Kiplinger Washington Editors.

Other ATE projects helped influence this work. The college visited the AIM Center at Sinclair Community College in Dayton, Ohio, and has pilot-tested several of Sinclair's instructional units. In addition, project staff participated in a curriculum development workshop at the New Jersey Center for Advanced Technological Education at Middlesex County College and applied this information in the scope and sequence and learning experiences developed for the DMT program.

Student Recruitment

There is a need to attract more students to manufacturing from under-represented groups (American Society of Training and Development 1993). If more technicians are to be enticed into the program, many of them must be female and minority students. The OSU-Okmulgee program has a strong representation of students with a Native American heritage and is reaching out to more female students. As the DMT program matures, staff are giving more attention to recruiting students from groups that typically do not enroll in technical education programs.

Students learn about the DMT program through a variety of sources. Simple informational recruiting methods include booths at tool shows and trade shows, programs at high schools and vocational-technical schools, showcases featuring OSU-Okmulgee technology, presentations at meetings and seminars, and brochures, including one aimed at underrepresented populations. Admissions counselors work with students and offer scholarships where appropriate.

Less traditional approaches draw other students. The OSU-Okmulgee Summer Manufacturing Academy for area middle and high school students—and county teachers—attracts young people who may not have considered manufacturing as a career. Another innovative approach is for present students to

Competencies. The curriculum content is composed of 24 competency areas in the categories of workplace effectiveness, personal productivity, technical competencies, and support skills. The advisory council has agreed that high-performance technicians need these skills and knowledge to span job descriptions and structural and cultural boundaries. The competency areas were derived from the input of a large group of leaders in manufacturing and business, from analysis of the literature, and from staff experience as employees, managers, employers, businesspersons, and vocational/technical teachers. Confirming the regional analysis, a comparison of DMT competencies with SCANS (1991) competencies and foundations finds an almost parallel conclusion.

Learning experiences. In solving authentic manufacturing problems and completing real manufacturing projects, the DMT learning experience has developed content that is innovative, transportable, meta-disciplinary, and action-oriented. Organized by segments, modules, and activities, the curriculum maintains flexibility in allowing learning experiences to be spontaneity-oriented (just-in-time).

Pilot-testing. Fourteen students who enrolled in the fall 1997 semester, 7 students who enrolled for the spring semester, and 10 students who enrolled for the fall 1998 semester have demonstrated the validity of the approach. Their commitment to learning and rapid progress has amazed intern companies, advisory board members, and faculty across the campus. DMT students have been described by intern companies as able to hit the ground running.

Recruitment and retention. Staff have recruited a larger proportion of minorities for DMT than exists in other technical programs at the college. The overall retention rate is over 80 percent, with 26 of the 32 students who originally enrolled in the program continuing their studies. Retention rates for other programs at the college average 50 percent. Class attendance is approximately 95 percent.

Industry relations. Approximately 40 businesses from Oklahoma, Missouri, Texas, and Kansas are serving on the DMT Advisory Board. Twice a year, these business leaders gather together to discuss and approve (or disapprove) DMT strategies, including curriculum objectives. Throughout the year, DMT faculty, staff, and students interact with these companies to find mutually beneficial projects/ideas, collaborate on field experiences, exchange knowledge, and work on other aspects of the program.

When we graduate, we will be high-performance technicians and will be able to go out and do tasks, solve problems, and work well because of what we have learned at DMT.

—DMT student

receive financial rewards when they are directly responsible for recruiting a new student.

The college also has on its campus a vocational-technical high school that can funnel students from the secondary manufacturing program to the college's DMT program. High school students can enroll concurrently in the college, then enter the college with advanced standing. Both institutions cost-share teacher expenses, some recruiting, transportation, and equipment. The high school pays the student's college tuition. Dual enrollment students have been more successful when they take college classes as a group.

Unexpected Outcomes

Perhaps the most important outcome has been that high-risk students succeed. This is attributable in large measure to the program's extensive application of close-learning communities, in which students help each other master competencies and faculty act as resources and advisors rather than authorities at arm's length.

At first, it was not obvious that the right educational process does not automatically result from the right curriculum. But eventually it became clear that much is dependent on the students, administration, and faculty.

Students. Students must understand that what they put into this program will be directly proportional to what they get from it. This implies a certain amount of maturity, and neither administrators nor facilitators can force maturity. Admissions requirements can be set to allow only seemingly mature students to enter the program—or the college can be patient with students as they mature while in the program.

Administration. Administrators must be supportive and act as role models. This means they must allow facilitators and students to take risks. It might also mean "walking the talk" of democratic processes for decision making.

Faculty. The program requires major shifts in faculty approaches to instruction, shifts that many faculty must struggle to accommodate. Effective faculty ultimately are able to make the shift from operating in a closed, independent, isolated environment to working in an open, dependent, group decision-making setting. They also shift from the "sage on the stage" stance to one that converts the instructor to a facilitator who sets up the situations so that students can learn for themselves. DMT faculty become champions of students, not merely sorters of students (into A students, B students, etc.). They switch from teaching to guiding. The same approach is advocated for staff development. For example, it does not make sense to lecture to facilitators about how not to be lecturers.

An unexpected outcome relates to the program's effect on general education. The program approach required the integration of general educational components with technical instruction. Bundling these traditionally discrete parts is much talked about in education circles but little practiced. Project staff had to plow new ground. To help with the integration of general education, specialists from many departments—including history, government, technical writing, mathematics, science, communication arts, accounting, marketing, and public relations—participated. They were especially helpful in determining the competencies to be woven into the projects and the methods used to assess those competencies. They also worked to satisfy traditionalists who require transcripts that include courses and grades.

The high level of student interest surprised faculty. Students arrived at class on time 97 percent of the time and attended every day from 7:30 a.m. to 3:30 p.m. Some continued working as late as 7:30 at night on their projects and volunteered for all kinds of extra duties, such as conducting the

I'm not much into competition anymore; I'm into cooperation. When you have competition, you have losers.

—Faculty member

OSU-Okmulgee's small class sizes helped personalize the learning experiences for me as a student. The OSU-Okmulgee faculty provided learning experiences I needed to build confidence for success in a non-traditional field for women. The academic clubs and social activities gave me the opportunity to meet people and network when looking for my first job after college. The Graduate Performance Guarantee I received, in addition to the associate in applied science degree, helped confirm my qualifications when I began my new career.

—A.A.S. program graduate

advisory council meetings or going on a recruitment visit to a local high school.

Faculty and students are much closer than in traditional programs. In the DMT learning community, faculty and students work as peers. Faculty are members of the learning teams, working closely with individuals and small groups, creating mutually respectful relationships, which carry over into a variety of social circumstances.

Recognition

Students in the OSU-Okmulgee program have received nearly as many honors and accolades as the college staff. One student was featured in an issue of Pro-Fab Inc.'s company publication, where he was interning. Another student published an article about the DMT experience even before graduation. A team of DMT students—participating for the first time—earned second place in the 1999 Oklahoma State SkillsUSA-VICA manufacturing contest. Two DMT students received scholarships from Tulsa-area manufacturing associations. Numerous local newspaper articles featured the DMT program and its students.

An OSU-Okmulgee faculty member was invited to publish articles about the DMT program and the learning paradigm. Administrators

and faculty presented at a range of conferences, including those sponsored by the National Science Foundation, the American Society for Engineering Education, the Midwestern Educational Research Association, the Tulsa Manufacturer's Association, the American Association of Community Colleges (Workforce Development Institute), the Rocky Mountain Educational Research Association, and the American Vocational Association. Others presented at the Best Practices in Manufacturing Conference in Cleveland, the Learning Paradigm Conference in San Diego, and the TransAtlantic Technology and Training Alliance (TA3) in Scotland.

College Commitment

The college supports the DMT program in the same way it supports all of its other technology programs, but it also has provided special assistance, including the full costs of all faculty and administrators associated with program's development.

The home of the program is in the newest campus facility, the Reynolds Technology Center. DMT occupies 17,000 square feet of the lower level of the 56,000-square-foot center. The college equipped the program with more than $1.5 million in state-of-the-art equipment that includes the only stereolithography machine owned and operated by an educational institution in the region, as well as plastic injection molding, Computerized Numeric Control (CNC) machines, robotics and other manufacturing equipment.

What's Next?

This program was institutionalized from its inception. DMT is a continuation of an ongoing manufacturing program, in the same facilities and using the same staff as it would without National Science Foundation support. Rather than develop a new program, the college revolutionized an existing program with these funds. Further, the use of faculty from other disciplines to create just-in-time learning strengthened the acceptance of and commitment to the program throughout the college community.

Already in progress is an endeavor to progressively expand DMT principles across the OSU-Okmulgee campus. DMT faculty and administrators will actively aid other colleges attempting to implement similar programs.

If we don't grow our own, we won't have the workers we need. I want all the interns I can get. This is the wave of the future if we want to keep manufacturing in the United States.
—*Manufacturing supervisor, Oklahoma City*

Materials Produced by the Program

The Distinctive Manufacturing Technology program produced a number of useful materials including brochures, flyers, and fact sheets that are available upon request. They include:

What is distinctive manufacturing technology? 1998 (July). Okmulgee: Oklahoma State University-Okmulgee.

Distinctive manufacturing technology program. 1998. Okmulgee: Oklahoma State University-Okmulgee.

Graduate performance guarantee.

Competency areas for distinctive manufacturing technology.

Creating sound bites.

Life-cycle design: Student's and instructor's guide.

Distinctive manufacturing technology: Curriculum development guide.

Distinctive manufacturing technology: Segment 1.

Field experiences for distinctive manufacturing technology.

Dimensions of teaching and learning.

DMT competency areas and priorities.

Distinctive manufacturing technology

program: Associate in applied science degree. 1998. Okmulgee: Oklahoma State University-Okmulgee.

Publications produced include:

Elliott, J. D. 1999. The DMT experience: Pro/Engineer in the university. *PRO-E: The Magazine* (July/August).

Shuler, Paul. (Forthcoming). *Barr and Tagg's learning paradigm and DMT.* Los Angeles: ERIC Clearinghouse for Community Colleges.

Shuler, Paul. (Forthcoming). *What DMT faculty have to say about the learning paradigm's real world implementation.* Los Angeles: ERIC Clearinghouse for Community Colleges.

References

American Society for Training and Development. 1993. *Building the technical workforce of tomorrow.* Alexandria, VA.

Ashcraft, Mark. 1994. *Human memory and cognition.* New York: HarperCollins College Publishers.

Bailey, T. 1990. Jobs of the future and the skills they will require: New thinking on an old debate. *American Educator* 14 (1).

Baxter, M., and J. Young. 1982. What do employers expect from high school graduates? *N.A.A.S.P. Bulletin* 66.

Buchanan, J. 1990, November. *Alaska youth: Ready for work, a call to action.* Anchorage: Alaska's Youth: Ready for Work.

Buck L. L., and R. K. Barrick. 1987. They're trained but are they employable? *Vocational Education Journal* 62 (5).

Busse, Roger. 1992. The new basics: Today's employers want the three R's and so much more. *Vocational Education Journal* 67 (5).

Crow, Steven. 1998. Making collaboration work:

A challenge for the commission. *NCA Quarterly,* 72 (4) (spring).

Drucker, Peter. 1986. Goodbye to the old personnel department. *Wall Street Journal,* 22 May: 30.

Dykman, Ann. 1997. The great college divide. *Techniques* (February).

Graham, S. A., E. Vitale, and M. L. Schenck. 1991. Developing methodologies to integrate content and behavioral skills: A pragmatic approach to curriculum design. *Community/Junior College Quarterly of Research and Practice* 15 (3).

Greathouse, Lillian. 1986. More than technical skills needed for career success. *Business Education Forum* (November).

Lankard, Bettina. 1990. Employability: The fifth basic skill. *ERIC Digest* (Columbus, Ohio, ERIC Clearinghouse on Adult, Career, and Vocational Education) no.104. (ED 325 659).

Nagle, Rhea. 1987. The ideal job candidate of the 21st century. *Journal of Career Planning and Employment* 47.

Naisbett, John. 1986. *The new American boom.* Washington, D.C.: Kiplinger Washington Editors.

National Science Foundation. 1993, July. *Gaining the competitive edge: Critical issues in science and engineering technician education.* Washington, D.C.

O'Banion, Terry. 1997. *Creating more learning-centered community colleges.* Mission Viego, Calif.: League for Innovation in the Community College.

Packer, Arnold. 1992. Taking action on the SCANS report. *Educational Leadership* 49 (6).

SCANS (Secretary's Commission on Achieving Necessary Skills). 1991, April. *Learning a living: A blueprint for high performance.* Executive Summary. Washington, D.C.: U.S. Department of Labor.

Shearer M., and R. Eadie. 1987. Employability skills: Keys to success. *Thrust* 17 (2).

Stasz, C., K. Ramsey, R. Eden, J. DaVanzo, H. Farris, and M. Lewis. 1993. *Classrooms that work: Teaching generic skills in academic and vocational settings.* Santa Monica, Calif.: RAND Corporation.

U.S. Department of Labor. 1993. *Teaching the SCANS competencies.* Washington, D.C.: Secretary's Commission on Achieving Necessary Skills.

Seminole Community College
Sanford, Florida

Introductory College Physics/
21st Century (ICP/21)

▶ **FOCUS**
▶ Introductory college physics curriculum with media-based modules and technology
▶ Hands-on problem solving

College Environment

Seminole Community College (SCC) is located in metropolitan Orlando, just east of Lake Mary and south of Sanford. The 200-acre main campus preserves the best of what Florida has to offer—rolling countryside, stately pines, moss-laden oaks, and a crystal clear, spring-fed lake. A diverse mission and academic offerings make Seminole the most comprehensive of the 28 Florida community colleges. It is the 13th largest in the state, serving 28,507 students annually. Twenty-nine is the median age of the student population, which is 53 percent female.

Students can take their first steps toward a college degree or learn skills equal to the rapidly changing business and professional world. The wide-ranging curriculum is shaped to meet the needs of high school graduates just beginning their educational journey, business professionals requiring new skills, technicians seeking updated information certification, workers learning completely new skills, and even hobbyists who want to learn more about a subject close to their heart. The college offers more than 4,000 day, evening, weekend, and distance learning classes. The associate in arts (A.A.) degree, with its 30 majors, attracts 28.2 percent of SCC students, with the 29 associate in science (A.S.) degree programs capturing 20.2 percent.

Seminole Community College
100 Weldon Boulevard
Sanford, FL 32773-6199
Ph: 407/328-2009
www.seminole.cc.fl.us
President: E. Ann McGee

Contacts
Alexander Dickison, Principal Investigator
Department of Physical Sciences
Seminole Community College
Ph: 407/328-2202
Fax: 407/328-2238
E-mail: dickisoa@mail.seminole.cc.fl.us

Marvin Nelson, Co-principal Investigator
Green River Community College
Auburn, WA
Ph: 253/833-9111 x4351
Fax: 253/288-3464
E-mail: mnelson@grcc.ctc.edu

Pearley Cunningham, Co-principal Investigator
Community College of Allegheny County, South Campus
Pittsburgh, PA
Ph: 412/469-6299
Fax: 412/469-6371
E-mail: pcunning@ccac.edu

Program Web Address
www.acd.ccac.edu/icp21

College prep students account for 8 percent of the total student population by program area.

Career and continuing education courses are available for business and technical professionals who need new skills and want to keep pace with changes in the workplace. The college's adult education programs include adult basic education, adult high school, general educational development (GED), and English for speakers of other languages (ESOL). Certificate programs provide occupational training in 32 different career areas, and community education courses offer a multitude of subjects that appeal to a learner's special interests, hobbies, or just plain curiosity.

Numerous special offerings complement these programs, including an honors seminar and the liberal studies program with its challenging curriculum for students with diverse backgrounds and interests. The science merit diploma program has a rigorous biological and physical science curriculum recommended by universities for science and engineering majors. Students interested in pursuing a certificate or associate degree program may choose the college's accelerated track, Speedegree. They can earn a degree in 12 to 18 months or a certificate in 12 months or less. The International Cooperative Studies in Mexico program provides a vehicle for students to travel abroad on educational expeditions to earn college and cooperative education credits. SCC also has junior- and senior-level classes on campus for individuals who have earned an associate degree. The University of Central Florida offers classes in arts and sciences, business, education, engineering, and health and public services.

I liked the interactive labs. They are much better than just reading the textbook. The class was fun.

—Student

SCC students graduating with an A.A. degree are guaranteed admission to a four-year Florida university and can begin junior-level coursework in any of more than 30 majors. SCC students who move on to four-year universities perform better academically, on average, than third-year university students. Graduates from specialized career and technical programs, such as nursing, engineering, computer and automotive technology, often find themselves in high demand as they enter the workforce.

SCC uses today's technology to transform homes and offices into 21st century classrooms. The Internet and television convey information to students whose business or personal demands do not permit them to actually visit a campus. All that is required is a computer with Internet access or a television and VCR. Distance learning students can set their own schedule and follow their instructor's syllabus for homework assignments and test dates.

SCC's technical and career programs are developed with the active and enthusiastic participation of leading Florida businesses. To that end, SCC's Information Technology Taskforce—with representatives from the I-4 High Technology Corridor Council, AT&T, Lucent Technologies, Lockheed Martin, Convergys, Siemens Telecom Networks, Florida Power Corporation, and the University of Central Florida—addresses issues of the day while keeping an eye to the new millennium. By establishing partnerships with the college, industry leaders such as Novell, Microsoft, Siemens Telecom Networks, and Ford Motor Company are virtually guaranteed a continual flow of competently trained employees. And because the partnering companies helped to develop the curricula, SCC graduates quickly become productive members of the corporate culture—eliminating the need for costly retraining. Two new A.S. degree programs—multimedia technology, and business administration and management—illustrate the positive outcomes of collaboration with the local

Students exploring the relationship between frequency, period, displacement, and amplitude in the wave/sound module.

*Doing the actual labs helped me
understand the subject better.*

—Student

business community to fill a void in the workforce. Students gain valuable practical, hands-on experience, complementing theoretical classroom instruction, as employers eagerly offer internships and co-op positions each semester.

The Seminole Community College Tech Prep program, in collaboration with the Seminole County Public Schools, is a seamless high-tech, high-standard curriculum spanning the last two years of high school. A student's Tech Prep training concludes after a two-year program of practical and theoretical study at SCC and culminates in an A.S. degree. According to state and national statistics, the fastest-growing fields and the jobs needing the most employees are largely technical in nature. SCC offers the training needed in high-knowledge, high-wage technical careers.

The SCC Business and Industry Support Center (BISC) makes it easy for businesses to offer professional development and update training. SCC provides everything from customer service training to computer classes designed to help transition workers to new or different software. BISC can offer a complete training solution or can support a company's existing training department as a training partner.

Program Profile

With its Advanced Technological Education grant, Seminole Community College has developed an innovative curriculum called Introductory College Physics/21st Century (ICP/21). It is targeted at students in medical and engineering technology programs, although it is suitable for all college students. The algebra/trigonometry-based course had its genesis in the *Principles of Technology Modules,* a series of modules developed by a National Science Foundation project in the 1970s. The course is available in printed copy as well as in IBM and MAC versions on CD-ROM. The CD-ROM versions allow the instructor to edit material before printing them for classroom use, thus permitting flexibility to adjust them to suit specific classes.

Faculty can pick and choose portions of the full program for presentation. The curriculum incorporates the new findings in cognitive science to enhance student learning. The modules introduce activities designed to build a student's conceptual understanding and capacity to make connections between and among related ideas.

ICP/21 attempts to show students that physics has everyday applications. Each module in the new curriculum uses current technological devices to introduce physics concepts. The use of this equipment motivates students and helps them to see the connections between physics and their chosen fields. The course maintains a rigor that makes it transferable to universities.

It emphasizes a hands-on approach and introduces major concepts of introductory physics. Although it covers less material than traditional introductory physics courses, it investigates the concepts in greater depth. The program is based on the philosophy that it is more important for students to fully understand fewer basic concepts and have confidence in applying them to new situations than it is for students to be exposed to numerous ideas that are neither understood nor remembered.

Each module includes some key features:

Active engagement of students: The need for lectures is greatly reduced. Most classroom time is devoted to laboratories, work sheet activities, and discussions among students.

Two-track curriculum option: One track incorporates the use of high technology equipment—MBL (microcomputer-based lab) and

Students exploring how forces add together in the force module.

PARTNERS

Green River Community College, Washington. Home to a co-principal investigator who is a module writer and editor, the college serves as a test site for the electricity module.

Community College of Allegheny County-South Campus, Pennsylvania. Home to a co-principal investigator who is a module writer and editor, the college is a test site for the heat module.

Other college and university module development and test sites. Additional colleges: Lake Sumter Community College, Florida (motion module); Seminole Community College, Florida (forces module); Pennsylvania State University, Beaver Campus (torque module); University of Washington (optics module); University of Nebraska and Omaha Westside High School, Nebraska (modern module); Northern Oklahoma College (work/energy module); Middlesex Community College, Massachusetts (waves/sound module); Cloud County Community College, Kansas (magnetism module); Tool Box, Nebraska (math topics, graphing, review topics for all modules).

CBL (calculator-based, multimedia, computer analysis of data)—in the laboratory and classroom. The other track allows instructors to teach the same concepts using traditional equipment.

Quantitative problem solving: Instructors emphasize procedures and problem-solving strategies—not just getting the "right answers." Students use multiple representations for most problems and are able to tie together the knowledge gained by analyzing a problem from pictorial, physical, graphical, and mathematical perspectives.

Learning cycles: Students actively test their own conceptual understandings of the natural world. If their conceptual models do not work, they are led to the construction of a more accepted scientific model that does work. Each module contains three to five sections. The sections build on their mathematical sophistication.

This is the first class I've ever had that reaches real problem-solving skills. Nothing is hand-fed to the students.

—Student

Developed by 10 collaborating community colleges and universities across the nation, the modules were validated by more than 20 technical education instructors and industry employees who assessed the accuracy of the real-world problems and examples. The NSF visiting team of university and community college experts also provided advice and counsel on project directions and reviewed each module.

Why This Approach?

The college's several Tech Prep programs—including electronics, automotive, telecommunications, computers, and civil and architectural engineering technology—require physics. Although students should begin to take physics prior to high school graduation, they do not always do so. Experience has shown that too many of these "techies" do not come to college fully prepared for college coursework or for physics. This makes the introductory college physics course particularly important. However, community college students, especially those enrolled in technology programs, want to know why they need to take physics. These students tend to be older, have outside family and job responsibilities, and are highly focused on their individual career goals. They resent course requirements that do not appear to contribute directly to their preparation for jobs and careers. To be effective for this audience, course materials and instructional strategies must connect the discipline to its application in the work world.

This program responds to these circumstances by using physics applications, problems, and examples found in industry and medicine. Through them, students quickly understand that physics is an important underpinning of their field of study. The applications are shaped so they are not overly complicated and fit the simple models of introductory college physics.

The modules cut through a lot of heavy stuff in the book—made it easier to see basics.

—Student

Influences on Program Development

Physics educators include pathfinders who take recent findings about how students learn physics and create methods and strategies to improve instruction. ICP/21 program writers and editors took pathfinders' ideas and experimented with them to create the modules and to test them in the classroom. These cutting-edge ideas were modified and adapted to meet the unique needs and circumstances of two-year college technology students.

The ICP/21 pathfinders came from a variety of places: Arnold Arons and Lillian McDermott, University of Washington; John Clement, University of Massachusetts; Robert Fuller, University of Nebraska; Fred Goldberg, San Diego State University, California; Priscilla Laws, Dickinson College, Pennsylvania; David Maloney, Indiana-Purdue University; Frederick Reif, Carnegie-Mellon University, Pennsylvania; Ronald Thornton, Tufts University, Massachusetts; Cindy Schwarz, Vassar College, New York; David Sokoloff, University of Oregon; Melvin Steinberg, Smith College, Massachusetts; Alan VanHeuvelen, Ohio State University; and Dean Zollman, Kansas State University. Max Kurtz of the Ztek Corporation in Kentucky provided guidance to format the modules for use on CD-ROMs, in printed copy, and on the Internet. The American Association of Physics Teachers permitted SCC to use its Physics of Technology modules.

Student Recruitment

Since the ICP/21 modules are designed for use in required first-year physics courses, no special recruitment effort was necessary to attract students.

Unexpected Outcomes

There has been a strong interest in ICP/21 among instructors teaching technical physics. It appears that many want to design a course that fits the new expectations of employees, accrediting agencies, and educational reform.

MAJOR ACHIEVEMENTS

Widespread partnerships. Involved 20 community college and university physics instructors at 10 different institutions across the country. Each site produced one module.

Advisory committees. Organized two project advisory committees (including a national visiting committee) and developed an advisory committee manual and guidelines. These committees allow input from industry, technical instructors, and high school teachers.

Standardized format. Developed a format for the modules that was followed by all writers.

Instructional models. Prepared and classroom-tested 10 modules, including CD-ROM application.

Dissemination. Shared information through presentations, workshops, and prepared papers.

Most students enjoy and appreciate the hands-on approach that puts lectures at a minimum. Some, however, feel uncomfortable with the problem-solving approach. The use of a learning cycle that requires them to develop their own models and then, using multiple representations, to express themselves is more work then they are used to. Most develop an appreciation of this approach by the end of the course, but a small minority would still prefer the straightforward "plug and chug" approach.

An unexpected challenge was the difficulty in finding real-world problems and examples that fit the simple models used in introductory physics. Most technical problems use more complicated models. Often when appropriate examples are identified, employers—driven by competition—are reluctant to share their real-world data.

Recognition

A number of papers, presentations, and technical assistance opportunities arose from Seminole's ICP/21 program. As a mentor in the Phi Theta Kappa faculty enhancement and curriculum development project, the principal investigator worked with Bronx Community College in New York, Fox Valley Technical College in Wisconsin, and Jefferson State College in Alabama from 1996 to 1998. Presentations on integrating physics curriculum and new technologies were presented at the National Conference of College Teaching and Learning and twice at summer meetings of the American Association of Physics Teachers. Project staff gave two workshops at the Introductory Physics Conference for Two-Year Colleges (Lee College, Texas, 1997; Joliet Junior College, Illinois, 1998), and another at the American Association of Physics Teachers Summer Meeting (University of Nebraska, 1998). Articles about ICP/21 appeared in publications of the American Physical Society and the American Association of Physics Teachers.

College Commitment

The college has made some considerable accommodations for the project. In addition to providing staff time, office space, and equipment, SCC covered half the cost of the sophisticated computer equipment required by the program's technical writer. The college also made it possible for key program staff to participate in meetings and workshops necessary for smooth program development. The availability of campus space and college vans was an added plus.

Leveraged Funds

The ATE grant inspired two of the college test sites—Green River Community College and the Community College of Allegheny County—to join Seminole Community College in providing funds for computer hardware and software, laboratory equipment, travel, and meetings. Ztek Corporation provided technical expertise in putting the modules into the correct format and on CD-ROM.

What's Next?

SCC plans to conduct extensive field-testing of the ICP/21 modules and to disseminate them broadly.

Materials Produced by the Program

The modules were prepared for classroom use during the 2000-01 school year. Faculty workshops scheduled during spring and summer 2000 will prepare teachers to use ICP/21 material. The module titles and descriptions are listed below:

Module 1: Motion
Uses an industrial production line to develop the concepts of position, distance, displacement, speed, velocity, and acceleration. The final section, Section 4, explores two-dimensional motion, which requires the use of vectors.

Module 2: Forces
Uses a robotic arm on a production line and a patient who must undergo traction of her leg to develop the concepts of statics and dynamics. Section 5 goes into two-dimensional situations that require mathematical use of vectors.

Module 3: Torque
Uses the robotic arm and levers of the human body to teach about torque and rotational static equilibrium. The end of the module introduces a quick overview of rotational dynamics.

Module 4: Work/Energy
Uses prosthesis devices as the catalyst that forms the need for a new model using work, energy, and power.

Module 5: Waves/Sound
Uses active noise control in industry to teach the concepts behind waves and sound.

Module 6: Heat
Uses an overheating electronic device by a power transistor to illustrate the underlying concepts behind temperature and heat. The optional last section allows students to design their own house, determine its thermal resistance, and estimate how much it would cost to heat and cool it during the year.

Module 7: Electricity
Introduces the basics of direct current circuits, starting with the concepts of charge, current, resistance, and voltage. Developing the ability to trouble shoot some basic electrical circuits provides the motivation to learn how circuits work.

Module 8: Magnetism
Development and production at toy factory of several prototypes, including WNBA "Barbie" and USA "Soccer Barbie", leads to the development of the concepts behind magnetic fields and electromagnetic induction.

Module 9: Optics
Introduces geometrical optics to understand the working of the human eye and microscope.

Module 10: Modern
Uses several different real-world motivations: (1) the photoelectric eye used on doors and conveyor belts is used to understand the photoelectric effect; (2) the bar code reader helps students explore basic atomic theory; and (3) the optional final section leads to understanding the solid state laser.

Bibliography

Advanced Technology Environmental Education Center. 1996. *Defining environmental technology.* Bettendorf, Iowa: Advanced Technology Environmental Education Center.

Advanced Technology Environmental Education Center. 1995. *Partnering to build a quality workforce: Critical issues in environmental technology education at two-year colleges.* Bettendorf, Iowa: Advanced Technology Environmental Education Center.

Andrews, Hans A., and John Allen. 1992. CIM (computer integrated manufacturing) in higher education: A partnership with IBM. *Community Services Catalyst* (spring): 7-10.

Baldwin, Fred D. 1996. Putting the community first. *Appalachia* (September-December): 12-15.

Biermann, Carol. 1996. The community college: Uniquely qualified to meet the challenges of today's science students. *Community Review* 14: 45-51.

Brodsky, Stanley. 1990. *Campus seminars/workshops to improve recruitment and retention of women and minorities in associate degree science and engineering technology programs.* Final report. New York: City University of New York Institute for Research and Development in Occupational Education.

Brodsky, Stanley. 1989. *Staff development to improve recruitment and retention of women and minorities in associate degree science and engineering technology programs.* New York: City University of New York Institute for

Research and Development in Occupational Education.

Burton, Lawrence, and Carin Celebuski. 1995. *Technical education in 2-year colleges.* HES Survey no. 17. Arlington, Va.: Division of Science Resources Studies, National Science Foundation.

CAUSE. 1995. Professional development. In *New opportunities for partnering.* Proceedings of the 1994 CAUSE Annual Conference. Boulder, Colo.: CAUSE.

Claire, Susan. 1992. *How to start a math engineering and science achievement (MESA) center at a community college.* Aptos, Calif.: Cabrillo College MESA Center.

Di Bendetto, Victoria, and Rachel Ortiz. 1994. *Women in technology: Project opportunity.* El Paso, Tex.: El Paso Community College. ERIC, ED 373 841.

Directorate for Education and Human Resources. 1995. *Advanced technological education program 1994 awards and activities.* Arlington, Va.: National Science Foundation.

Directorate for Education and Human Resources. 1996. *Advanced technological education program 1995 awards and activities.* Arlington, Va.: National Science Foundation.

Directorate for Education and Human Resources. 1997. *Advanced technological education program 1996 awards and activities.* Arlington, Va.: National Science Foundation.

Directorate for Education and Human Resources. 1998. *Advanced technological education program 1997 awards and activities*. Arlington, Va.: National Science Foundation.

Directorate for Education and Human Resources. 1995. *National science foundation activities in support of two-year college science, mathematics, engineering, and technology education*. Fiscal year 1994 highlights. Arlington, Va.: National Science Foundation.

Directorate for Education and Human Resources. 1996. *National science foundation activities in support of two-year college science, mathematics, engineering, and technology education*. Fiscal year 1995 highlights. Arlington, Va.: National Science Foundation.

Directorate for Education and Human Resources. 1997. *National science foundation activities in support of two-year college science, mathematics, engineering and technology education*. Fiscal year 1996 highlights. Arlington, Va.: National Science Foundation.

Directorate for Education and Human Resources. Advisory Committee to the National Science Foundation. 1996. *Shaping the future: New expectations for undergraduate education in science, mathematics, engineering, and technology*. Washington, D.C.: National Science Foundation. ERIC, ED 404 158.

Fabricant, Mona, and Haya Adner. 1989. *Women in science and technology*. Bayside, N.Y.: Queensborough Community College. ERIC, ED 325 143.

Greenberg, Richard. 1998. Build it and they will come. *Techniques: Making Education and Career Connections* (May): 16-19.

Johnson, Larry. 1996. *Common ground: Exemplary community college and corporate partnerships*. Mission Viejo, Calif.: League for Innovation in the Community College.

Johnson, Scott D., and Rita McDonough Fischbach. 1992. *Teaching problem solving and technical mathematics through cognitive apprenticeship at the community college level*. Berkeley, Calif.: National Center for Research in Vocational Education.

Jones, Enid B. 1993. *Lessons for the future: Minorities in math, science, and engineering at community colleges*. Report of a Roundtable 13-14 August, 1992. Washington, D.C.: American Association of Community Colleges. ERIC, ED 363 366.

Koltai, Leslie, and Michael Wilding. 1991. *The status of science, engineering, and mathematics education in community, technical, and junior colleges*. Washington, D.C.: American Association of Community and Junior Colleges.

Langshort, Scott A. 1997. Changing the channel: Community colleges in the information age. *Community College Review* (winter): 55-72.

Loucks-Horsley, Susan, et al. 1996. The role of community colleges in the professional development of science teachers. *Journal of College Science Teaching* (November): 130-34.

Mahoney, James R., and Lynn Barnett. 1998. *Developing technicians: Successful international systems*. Washington, D.C.: American Association of Community Colleges. ERIC, ED 424 880.

Maricopa Advanced Technology Center. 2000. *Broadening the impact: A profile and update of national science foundation sponsored centers of excellence and selected projects in the advanced technological education program*. Tempe, Ariz.: Maricopa County Community College District.

National Council for Occupational Education Diversity Task Force. 1996. *Preparing a diverse workforce for the twenty-first century*. Columbus, Ohio: National Council for Occupational Education.

Packer, Arnold. 1994. *An associate degree in high-performance manufacturing*. Final report.

Indiana, Penn.: Pennsylvania Association of Developmental Educators.

Quimbita, Grace. 1991. *Preparing women and minorities for careers in math and science: The role of the community colleges.* Los Angeles: ERIC Clearinghouse for Junior Colleges. ERIC, ED 333 943.

Stout, Dorothy LaLonde. 1993. Collaboration between professional societies and two-year schools. *Journal of College Science Teaching* (November): 74-75.

Taylor, Marilyn J., et al. 1997. Women who say "yes" when science says "no": Their lessons for future students and teachers. Paper presented at the 49th Annual Meeting of the American Association of Colleges for Teacher Education, Phoenix, Ariz., 26 February–1 March. ERIC, ED 405 340.

Waintraub, Jack L. 1997. Redesigning engineering technology education: The New Jersey center for Advanced Technological Education. *Industry and Higher Education* 11 (4): 249-52 (August).

Appendix A
ATE Centers of Excellence

Bellevue Community College
NorthWest Center for Emerging Technologies
(NWCET)
3000 Landerholm Circle, SE
Bellevue, Washington 98007-6484
www.nwcet.bcc.edu
Focus: Information Technology

Chemeketa Community College
Northwest Center for Sustainable Resources (NCSR)
4000 Lancaster Drive, NE
Salem, Oregon 97309-7070
www.ncsr.org
Focus: Environmental Science

Eastern Iowa Community College District
Advanced Technology Environmental Education
Center (ATEEC)
500 Belmont Road
Bettendorf, Iowa 52722
www.ateec.com
Focus: Environmental Technology

Maricopa County Community College District
Maricopa Advanced Technology Education Center
(MATEC)
2323 West 14th Street, Suite 402
Tempe, Arizona 85281
http://matec.org
Focus: Microelectronics Manufacturing

Middlesex County College
New Jersey Center for Advanced Technological
Education (NJCATE)
2600 Woodbridge Avenue
Edison, New Jersey 08818
www.mccc.edu/njcate
Focus: Engineering Technology

Monterey Peninsula College
Marine Advanced Technology Education Center
(MATE)
980 Fremont Street
Monterey, California 93940
www.marinetech.org
Focus: Marine Technology

San Francisco Community College District
National Center for Biotechnology Education–
BioLink
1855 Folsom Street, Suite 643
San Francisco, California 94103
www.bio-link.org
Focus: Biotechnology

Sinclair Community College &
University of Dayton
Advanced Integrated Manufacturing Center–AIM
444 West Third Street
Dayton, Ohio 45402-1460
www.aimcenter.org
Focus: Manufacturing Engineering
Technology

South Carolina Technical College System
South Carolina ATE Center of Excellence–SC ATE
111 Executive Center Drive
Columbia, SC 29210
www.scate.org
> *Focus: Engineering Technology*

Springfield Technical Community College
Northeast Center for Telecommunications
Technology–NCTT
One Armory Square
Springfield, MA 01105
www.nctt.org
> *Focus: Telecommunications*

Texas State Technical College –Sweetwater
Southwest Consortium for the Advancement of
Technology in Education–SCATE
300 College Drive
Sweetwater, TX 79556
www.scate.net
> *Focus: Distance Learning*

Appendix B

ATE Funded Institutions: 1993-2000

Adirondack Community College, Glens Falls, NY

Alabama Southern Community College,
Monroeville, AL

Alamo Community College District, San Antonio
College, San Antonio, TX

Albuquerque Technical Vocational Institute,
Albuquerque, NM

Alvin Community College, Alvin, TX

Amarillo College, Amarillo, TX

American Association For Advancement Science,
Washington, DC

American Association of Community Colleges,
Washington, DC

American Association of Physics Teachers,
College Park, MD

American Chemical Society, Washington, DC

American Institute of Physics, College Park, MD

American Mathematical Association of Two-Year
Colleges, Memphis, TN

Athens Area Technical Institute, Athens, GA

Austin Community College, Austin, TX

Bay Shore Union Free School District,
Bay Shore, NY

Bellevue Community College, Bellevue, WA

Bergen Community College, Paramus, NJ

Berkshire Community College, Pittsfield, MA

Bismarck State College, Bismarck, ND

Brevard Community College, Cocoa, FL

Bronx Community College (CUNY), Bronx, NY

Broward Community College, Fort Lauderdale, FL

California State University-Hayward Foundation
Inc, Hayward, CA

Camden County College, Blackwood, NJ

Cape Cod Community College,
West Barnstable, MA

Capital Community Technical College,
Hartford, CT

Catonsville Community College, Catonsville, MD

Center for Image Processing in Education,
Tucson, AZ

Chattanooga State Technical Community College,
Chattanooga, TN

Chemeketa Community College, Salem, OR

City College of San Francisco, San Francisco, CA

Cleveland State University, Cleveland, OH

Cold Spring Harbor Laboratory, Cold Spring
Harbor, NY

College of the Desert, Palm Desert, CA

College of the Mainland, Texas City, TX

Collin County Community College, McKinney, TX

Colorado Community College & Occupational
Educational System, Denver, CO

Colorado State University, Fort Collins, CO

Concord Consortium, Concord, MA

Consortium for Advanced Manufacturing
International, Arlington, TX

Consortium for Mathematics & Its Applications
Inc, Lexington, MA

Consortium for Oceanographic Research and
Education, Inc, Washington, DC

CORD, Waco, TX

Cuesta College, San Luis Obispo, CA

Cypress College, Cypress, CA

Daytona Beach Community College,
Daytona Beach, FL

De Anza College, Cupertino, CA

Diné College, Tsaile, AZ

East Los Angeles College, Monterey Park, CA

Edison Industrial Systems Center, Toledo, OH

Edmonds Community College, Lynnwood, WA

Education Development Center, Newton, MA

Essex Community College, Essex, MD

Evergreen Valley College, San Jose, CA

Florida State University, Tallahassee, FL

Foothill College, Los Altos Hills, CA
Front Range Community College, Westminster, CO
Gadsden State Community College, Gadsden, AL
Geological Society of America Today, Boulder, CO
Georgetown University, Washington, DC
Global Wireless Education Consortium,
    St. Cloud, MN
Greenfield Community College, Greenfield, MA
Harold Washington College (City Colleges of
    Chicago), Chicago, IL
Harry S Truman College (City Colleges of
    Chicago), Chicago, IL
Harvard University, Cambridge, MA
Hawkeye Community College, Waterloo, IA
Hazardous Materials Training & Research
    Institute, Bettendorf, IA
Hazardous Materials Training & Research
    Center, Cedar Rapids, IA
Henry Ford Community College, Dearborn, MI
Hillsboro School District 1J, Hillsboro, OR
Hillsborough Community College, Tampa, FL
Hofstra University, Hempstead, NY
Houston Community College, Houston, TX
Huertas Junior College, Caguas, PR
Iḷisaġvik College, Barrow, AK
Illinois State University, Normal, IL
Indiana State University, Terre Haute, IN
Indiana University Bloomington, Bloomington, IN
Intelecom Intelligent Telecommunications,
    Pasadena, CA
Iowa State University, Ames, IA
J Sargent Reynolds Community College,
    Richmond, VA
Jefferson State Community College,
    Birmingham, AL
John C Calhoun State Community College,
    Decatur, AL
Johns Hopkins University, Baltimore, MD
Joliet Junior College, Joliet, IL
Jones County Junior College, Ellisville, MS
Kansas State University, Manhattan, KS
Keene State College, Keene, NH
Kings River Community College, Reedley, CA
Lac Courte Oreilles Ojibwa Community College,
    Hayward, WI
Lane Community College, Eugene, OR
Lee College, Baytown, TX
Los Rios Community College District,
    Sacramento, CA

Madison Area Technical College, Madison, WI
Maricopa County Community College District,
    Tempe, AZ
Mesa State College, Grand Junction, CO
Miami University Middletown, Middletown, OH
Michigan Technological University, Houghton, MI
Middlesex Community College, Bedford, MA
Middlesex County College, Edison, NJ
Milwaukee Area Technical College,
    Milwaukee, WI
Minnesota Riverland Technical College
    (Austin Campus), Austin, MN
Minnesota State Colleges & Universities,
    St. Paul, MN
MiraCosta College, Oceanside, CA
Mississippi Delta Community College,
    Moorhead, MS
Monroe Community College, Rochester, NY
Monterey Peninsula College, Monterey, CA
Monterey Peninsula Unified School District,
    Monterey, CA
Montgomery College, Rockville, MD
Moorpark College, Moorpark, CA
Moraine Valley Community College, Palos Hills, IL
Mott Community College, Flint, MI
Mount Hood Community College, Gresham, OR
Mount San Antonio College, Walnut, CA
Mount Wachusett Community College,
    Gardner, MA
MPR Associates, Berkeley, CA
Nashville State Technical Institute, Nashville, TN
National Alliance of Business, Washington, DC
National Association of Biology Teachers,
    Reston, VA
New England Board of Higher Education,
    Boston, MA
New Hampshire Technical College-Berlin,
    Berlin, NH
New Mexico State University - Dona Ana,
    Las Cruces, NM
New York City Tech College (CUNY),
    Brooklyn, NY
Norfolk State University, Norfolk, VA
North Carolina State Board of Community
    Colleges, Raleigh, NC
North Seattle Community College, Seattle, WA
Northern Illinois University, De Kalb, IL
Northwest Indian College, Bellingham, WA
Northwestern University, Evanston, IL

Oak Ridge Associated Universities, Oak Ridge, TN

Ohio University, Athens, OH

Oklahoma State University, Stillwater, OK

Old Dominion University Research Foundation,
	Norfolk, VA

Onondaga Community College (SUNY),
	Syracuse, NY

Partnership for Environmental Technology
	Education, Pleasanton, CA

Pasadena City College, Pasadena, CA

Pennsylvania College of Technology,
	Williamsport, PA

Pennsylvania State University,
	University Park, PA

Peralta Community College District Office,
	Oakland, CA

Phi Theta Kappa Headquarters, Jackson, MS

Piedmont Technical College, Greenwood, SC

Piedmont Virginia Community College,
	Charlottesville, VA

Pima County Community College, Tucson, AZ

Portland Community College, Portland, OR

Prince George's Community College, Largo, MD

Purdue University, West Lafayette, IN

Queensborough Community College (CUNY),
	New York, NY

Regents College, Albany, NY

Regional Technology Strategies, Chapel Hill, NC

Research Foundation of the City University of
	New York, New York, NY

Rochester Institute of Technology, Rochester, NY

Rock Valley College, Rockford, IL

Rose-Hulman Institute of Technology,
	Terre Haute, IN

Rutgers University New Brunswick,
	New Brunswick, NJ

San Diego City College, San Diego, CA

San Jose State University Foundation, San Jose, CA

Santa Fe Community College, Gainesville, FL

Seattle Community College South, Seattle, WA

Seminole Community College, Sanford, FL

Sinclair Community College, Dayton, OH

South Carolina Technical College System,
	Columbia, SC

Southeast Community College, Lincoln, NE

Southern Illinois University at Carbondale,
	Carbondale, IL

Springfield Technical Community College,
	Springfield, MA

Stark State College of Technology, Canton, OH

State College & University Systems of WV,
	Charleston, WV

SUNY at Stony Brook, Stony Brook, NY

SUNY College of Technology Alfred, Alfred, NY

Teachers College, Columbia University,
	New York, NY

TERC Inc, Cambridge, MA

Texas Engineering Experiment Station,
	College Station, TX

Texas State Technical College Sweetwater,
	Sweetwater, TX

Texas State Technical College-Waco, Waco, TX

Texas State Technical Institute-Harlingen Campus,
	Harlingen, TX

Thomas Nelson Community College,
	Hampton, VA

Traverse Bay Area Intermediate School District,
	Traverse City, MI

Tri-County Technical College, Pendleton, SC

Trident Technical Colleges, Charleston, SC

Tunxis Community-Technical College,
	Farmington, CT

University of Alaska Southeast Juneau Campus,
	Juneau, AK

University of California-Davis, Davis, CA

University of California-Santa Barbara,
	Santa Barbara, CA

University of Chicago, Chicago, IL

University of Cincinnati Main Campus,
	Cincinnati, OH

University of Connecticut, Storrs, CT

University of Georgia, Athens, GA

University of Hawaii Manoa, Honolulu, HI

University of Illinois at Chicago, Chicago, IL

University of Kentucky Research Foundation,
	Lexington, KY

University of Minnesota-Twin Cities,
	Minneapolis, MN

University of Nevada Desert Research Institute,
	Reno, NV

University of New Hampshire, Durham, NH

University of New Mexico, Albuquerque, NM

University of North Carolina at Chapel Hill,
	Chapel Hill, NC

University of Texas - Pan American, Edinburg, TX

University of Washington, Seattle, WA

Valencia Community College, Orlando, FL

Vermont Technical College, Randolph Center, VT

Wake Technical Community College, Raleigh, NC
Waukesha County Technical College,
    Pewaukee, WI
Wayne State University, Detroit, MI
Wentworth Institute of Technology, Boston, MA
West Valley-Mission Community College District,
    Saratoga, CA
Westark College, Fort Smith, AR
Western Wisconsin Technical College,
    La Crosse, WI
Wytheville Community College, Wytheville, VA
York Technical College, Rock Hill, SC

Appendix C
Advisory Committee

Representatives from business, government, and education met in Washington, D.C., in October 1998 to offer insights on how to tell the story of community colleges in the Advanced Technological Education program. They concluded that the best way was to document what a set of 13 programs set out to do, why and how they did it, who partnered with them, and what they accomplished, including unexpected outcomes. They recommended that the voices of students, instructors, and business partners complement each program narrative. The result is *The Learning Edge*. AACC thanks the following individuals who helped shape this book:

Todd Allen, Johnson & Johnson, Inc.
Sandra Byrne, National Institute of Standards and
    Technology
Patricia A. Cunniff, Prince George's Community
    College
Norris Dickard, U.S. Department of Education
Carol-Ann Meares, U.S. Department of Commerce
Elise Gross, Hillsborough Community College
Fredessa Hamilton, Anne Arundel Community
    College
Robert Mahaffey, National Association of
    Secondary School Principals
Rod Risley, Phi Theta Kappa
Aimee Rogstad, National Alliance of Business
Gerhard Salinger, National Science Foundation
Kendall Starkweather, Information Technology
    Education Association
Elizabeth Teles, National Science Foundation

Index

N